Cambridge Elements ≡

Elements in the Philosophy of Mathematics
edited by
Penelope Rush
University of Tasmania
Stewart Shapiro
The Ohio State University

MATHEMATICAL ANTI-REALISM AND MODAL NOTHINGISM

Mark Balaguer
California State University

CAMBRIDGE
UNIVERSITY PRESS

Shaftesbury Road, Cambridge CB2 8EA, United Kingdom

One Liberty Plaza, 20th Floor, New York, NY 10006, USA

477 Williamstown Road, Port Melbourne, VIC 3207, Australia

314–321, 3rd Floor, Plot 3, Splendor Forum, Jasola District Centre,
New Delhi – 110025, India

103 Penang Road, #05–06/07, Visioncrest Commercial, Singapore 238467

Cambridge University Press is part of Cambridge University Press & Assessment,
a department of the University of Cambridge.

We share the University's mission to contribute to society through the pursuit of
education, learning and research at the highest international levels of excellence.

www.cambridge.org
Information on this title: www.cambridge.org/9781009346016

DOI: 10.1017/9781009346030

First published 2022

A catalogue record for this publication is available from the British Library.

ISBN 978-1-009-34601-6 Paperback
ISSN 2399-2883 (online)
ISSN 2514-3808 (print)

Mathematical Anti-Realism and Modal Nothingism

Elements in the Philosophy of Mathematics

DOI: 10.1017/9781009346030
First published online: December 2022

Mark Balaguer
California State University

Author for correspondence: Mark Balaguer, mbalagu@calstatela.edu

Abstract: This Element defends mathematical anti-realism against an underappreciated problem with that view – a problem having to do with modal truthmaking. The first part develops mathematical anti-realism, defends that view against a number of well-known objections, and raises a less widely discussed objection to anti-realism – an objection based on the fact that (a) mathematical anti-realists need to commit to the truth of certain kinds of modal claims, and (b) it's not clear that the truth of these modal claims is compatible with mathematical anti-realism. The second part considers various strategies that anti-realists might pursue in trying to solve this modal-truth problem with their view, argues that there's only one viable view that anti-realists can endorse in order to solve the modal-truth problem, and argues that the view in question – which is here called modal nothingism – is true.

This Element also has a video abstract: www.cambridge.org/Philosophy of Mathematics_ Balaguer_abstract

Keywords: mathematical anti-realism, modality, error theory, truthmaking, abstract objects

ISBNs 9781009346016 (PB), 9781009346030 (OC)
ISSNs: 2399-2883 (online), 2514-3808 (print)

Contents

1 Introduction

Mathematical anti-realism is (somewhat roughly) the view that our mathematical theories don't provide true descriptions of mathematical objects (i.e., things like numbers and sets) because there are no such things as mathematical objects. The reason there are no mathematical objects, on this view, is that (a) if there were mathematical objects, they would be *abstract* objects – that is, nonphysical, nonmental, nonspatiotemporal objects – and (b) there are no abstract objects.

My central aim in this Element is to articulate what I think is an underappreciated problem for mathematical anti-realism – a problem having to do with the truthmaking of modal claims – and to develop and defend what I think is the only plausible solution to that problem.

In the first part of this Element, I'll provide a more thorough and precise articulation of mathematical anti-realism, I'll explain how I think that view should be developed, and I'll respond to a number of objections that you might raise against that view. But at the end of the first part, another objection will emerge, an objection based on the fact that (a) mathematical anti-realists need to commit to the truth of certain kinds of *modal* claims (i.e., *possibility* claims and/ or *necessity* claims and/or *counterfactuals*), and (b) it's not clear that the truth of these modal claims is compatible with mathematical anti-realism. In the second part of this Element, I'll run through the various strategies that anti-realists might pursue in trying to solve this modal-truth problem – that is, the problem of explaining how modal claims of the relevant kind could be true, given that mathematical anti-realism is also true – and I'll argue that there's only one viable view available to anti-realists here. I'll call this view *modal nothingism*, and I'll argue at the end of the second part that modal nothingism is true and that mathematical anti-realists can use this view to block the modal-truth objection to their view.

The first part of this Element consists of Sections 2–4. In Section 2, I'll do three things: I'll define mathematical realism and anti-realism; I'll distinguish three different versions of anti-realism, namely, paraphrase nominalism, deflationary-truth nominalism, and mathematical error theory; and I'll argue against paraphrase nominalism and deflationary-truth nominalism.

In Section 3, I'll respond to four objections to error theory. I'll spend most of my time responding to the worry that error theorists can't account for the factualness and objectivity of mathematics. After that, I'll respond to three more objections to error theory – a Moorean objection, a Lewisian objection, and a Quine-Putnam indispensability objection. During the course of the discussion, it will become clear that in order to respond to these objections, error theorists need to commit to the truth of certain kinds of *modal* claims.

In particular, I'll argue that they need to commit to the truth of either counter-factuals like

> [CF] If there had actually existed a plenitudinous realm of abstract objects, then it would have been the case that 3 was prime,

or necessitarian conditionals like

> [N] Necessarily, if there exists a plenitudinous realm of abstract objects, then 3 is prime.

Finally, at the end of Section 3, I'll point out that this creates a problem for error theory. For given that error theorists deny that there are abstract objects, it's not clear that they have access to any plausible account of how modal sentences like [CF] and [N] could be true.

In Section 4, I'll argue that, like error theorists, paraphrase nominalists and deflationary-truth nominalists need to commit to the truth of modal sentences like [CF] or [N], and so – again, like error theorists – they encounter the worry that they don't have access to any plausible account of how sentences like [CF] and [N] could be true, given that there are no such things as abstract objects.

The second part of this Element consists of Sections 5–8. In Section 5, I'll do two things. First, I'll introduce the two most prominent views of the semantics of ordinary modal sentences, namely, *the possible-worlds analysis* (which says, roughly, that ordinary modal sentences are claims about possible worlds) and *modal primitivism* (which says, roughly, that ordinary modal sentences involve primitive modal operators). Second, I'll introduce a principle that, prima facie, seems extremely plausible – namely, that for any true sentence S, *there's something about reality that makes S true* – and I'll point out that (a) given the plausibility of this principle, mathematical anti-realists owe an account of what it is about reality that makes modal sentences like [CF] and [N] true, and (b) given that anti-realists don't believe in abstract objects, it's not clear that they have access to any tenable view of what makes these modal sentences true.

In Section 6, I'll argue that, if they want to, mathematical anti-realists can endorse the possible-worlds analysis of ordinary modal discourse – if they also endorse a *modal error theory*; but I'll also argue that if they do this, then in order to account for the objectivity and factualness of our modal and mathematical discourse, they'll have to introduce novel primitive modal operators (i.e., primitive modal operators that aren't part of ordinary language), and moreover, they'll have to answer the truthmaking question for sentences involving these novel primitive modal operators. Thus, even if anti-realists endorse the possible-worlds analysis of ordinary modal discourse, they'll end up facing a modal truthmaking problem that's essentially equivalent to the modal truthmaking problem that they face if they endorse modal primitivism.

In Section 7, I'll turn to the question of whether mathematical anti-realists can solve the modal truthmaking problem if they endorse modal primitivism, and I'll argue that they don't seem to have any viable options here. More specifically, I'll argue that anti-realists don't have access to any plausible view of what makes ordinary modal sentences true. I'll do this by running through a number of options – including conventionalist views, essentialist views, and potentiality views – and arguing that none of the available views gives anti-realists what they need.

Finally, in Section 8, I'll argue that there's a way out of this problem for anti-realists. I'll do this by arguing against the assumption that every true sentence is made true by reality. More specifically, I'll argue that while our modal sentences are true – indeed, substantively and objectively true – *there's nothing about reality that makes them true*. I'll call this view *modal nothingism*, and in Section 8, I'll argue that it's true and that it gives mathematical anti-realists a solution to the modal truthmaking problem with their view.

MATHEMATICAL ANTI-REALISM

2 What Is Mathematical Anti-Realism?

2.1 Opening Remarks

In order to understand mathematical anti-realism, we first need to understand mathematical realism – because the former can be defined as simply the negation of the latter. Thus, I'll begin, in Section 2.2, by discussing mathematical realism (in particular, I'll define realism and explain why one might be attracted to the view, why one might be dissatisfied with it, and why the only tenable versions of realism involve a commitment to *platonism*). Then in Section 2.3, I'll define mathematical anti-realism, and I'll distinguish three different versions of that view – namely, paraphrase nominalism, deflationary-truth nominalism, and error theory. Finally, in Section 2.4, I'll argue against paraphrase nominalism and deflationary-truth nominalism.

2.2 Mathematical Realism

2.2.1 Mathematical Realism Defined

The best way to understand mathematical realism is to begin by thinking about mathematical theories (like Peano Arithmetic and Zermelo–Frankel set theory) and simple mathematical sentences (like '3 is prime'). Prima facie, '3 is prime' seems to be a true claim about a certain object, namely, the number 3; '3 is prime' seems analogous in this way to, for instance, 'Mars is round.' Just as the latter tells us that a certain object (Mars) has a certain property (roundness), so the former tells us that the object 3 has the property of being prime. And – again, prima facie – it seems that our mathematical theories give us a bunch of true claims about a bunch of objects; for example, Peano Arithmetic tells us that every natural number has a successor, and that there are infinitely many primes, and so on.

Mathematical realism is the view that these appearances (about theories like Peano Arithmetic and sentences like '3 is prime') are indeed true. More precisely, realism is the view that (a) there exist mathematical objects (e.g., numbers and sets), and (b) our mathematical theories (which include ordinary sentences like '3 is prime') provide true descriptions of these objects.

2.2.2 The Argument for Mathematical Realism

Consider the following argument:

[1] Mathematical sentences like '3 is prime' should be read at face value and, hence, as making straightforward claims about the nature of certain specific objects; for example, '3 is prime' should be read as being of the form '*Fa*' and, hence, as making a straightforward claim about the nature of the number 3. But

[2] If sentences like '3 is prime' should be read at face value, and if moreover they're true, then there must actually exist objects of the kinds that they're about; for example, if '3 is prime' makes a straightforward claim about the nature of the number 3, and if this sentence is literally true, then there must actually exist such a thing as the number 3. Moreover,

[3] Mathematical sentences like '3 is prime' *are* true. Therefore, from [1]–[3], it follows that

[4] There actually exist objects that mathematical sentences like '3 is prime' are about, and these sentences provide true descriptions of those objects; for example, the number 3 actually exists, and '3 is prime' provides a true description of that object.[1]

This argument is valid, and [4] is essentially equivalent to mathematical realism, and so if [1]–[3] are all true, then mathematical realism is also true. But, prima facie, it seems that [1]–[3] *are* true (and I'll articulate some arguments for these three premises in Sections 2.4, 3.2.1, and 3.4), and so it seems that mathematical realism is true.

---

[1] Arguments of this general kind have been given by many philosophers, most notably, Frege (1954, 1964).

2.2.3 Platonism as the Only Tenable Version of Mathematical Realism

We can define the following three versions of mathematical realism:

> *Physicalism (about mathematics)*: Our mathematical sentences and theories provide true descriptions of physical objects.

> *Psychologism (about mathematics)*: Our mathematical sentences and theories provide true descriptions of mental objects, presumably ideas in our heads.

> *Platonism (about mathematics)*: Our mathematical sentences and theories provide true descriptions of *abstract* objects (i.e., objects that are nonphysical, nonmental, nonspatiotemporal, unextended, and acausal).[2]

The most popular and prominent version of realism – and by far the *best* version, in my opinion – is platonism. This might be surprising. For the existence of abstract objects is extremely controversial – lots of people don't believe in them at all – and the existence of physical objects and mental objects (e.g., ideas in our heads) is relatively *un*controversial. So you might think that physicalism and psychologism are superior to platonism because they're metaphysically uncontroversial.

But there are very strong arguments against physicalism and psychologism (about mathematics). I won't go into any depth on these arguments here, but, very quickly, one argument against physicalism and psychologism is based on the claim that these two views falsely imply that the truth of our mathematical theories requires the existence of a gigantic infinity of physical or mental objects. Consider, for example, the following sentence (which is basically an informal version of Cantor's theorem):

> [CT] There are infinitely many transfinite cardinals that keep getting bigger and bigger without end.

Given this, we can argue against physicalism (or psychologism) as follows:

> If physicalism (or psychologism) were true, then the truth of [CT] would require the existence of a massive infinity of physical (or mental) objects. But (a) it seems likely that there just aren't that many physical (or mental) objects in the entire universe; and, more importantly, (b) the truth of [CT] actually *doesn't* depend on the existence of a massive infinity of physical (or mental) objects. If you rejected [CT] on the grounds that there aren't enough physical (or mental) objects in the entire universe to make [CT] true, that would just

---

[2] Platonist views have been defended by, among others, Frege (1953, 1964), Russell (1903), Quine (1961a, 1961b), Gödel (1964), Putnam (1971), Resnik (1997), Shapiro (1997), me (Balaguer 1998), Zalta (1999), Colyvan (2001), and on some interpretations, Maddy (1990). Physicalist views – or at least views with physicalist leanings – have been endorsed by Mill (1843), Kitcher (1984), and on some interpretations, Maddy (1990). Finally, views with psychologistic leanings have been endorsed by Brouwer (1983a, 1983b) and Heyting (1956).

show that you don't understand what [CT] *says*. In standard mathematical settings, [CT] just isn't a claim about physical (or mental) objects; it doesn't imply that there are *any* physical (or mental) objects, let alone a huge infinity of them. And this suggests that physicalism (and psychologism) are just false.

This argument is very quick, and there are various ways in which advocates of physicalism and psychologism might respond. But I don't think any of these responses succeed, and what's more, I think there are other good arguments against physicalism and psychologism. (For more arguments here, see Frege [1954, 1964], Resnik [1980], and me [Balaguer 1998, 2014].) But I won't run through the details of any of this here. Instead, I'll just assume that there are good arguments against physicalism and psychologism (about mathematics) – and, hence, that platonism is the only tenable version of realism. In other words, I'll assume – as is fairly standard in the literature these days – that if mathematical realism is true, then platonism is also true, so that our only viable options are platonism and anti-realism.

2.2.4 Why You Might Be Unhappy with Platonism (and, Hence, Attracted to Anti-Realism)

Given that the only tenable realist option is platonism, you might be inclined to reject that view. For you might simply not believe in abstract objects. Why? Well, not to put too fine a point on it, because you might think that abstract objects would be *metaphysically weird*, or *supernatural*, if they existed. Abstract objects are supposed to be wholly nonphysical and nonmental; they're not supposed to be *made* of anything; they're not supposed to be located anywhere (they're supposed to exist but not in space or time); and they're supposed to be wholly unextended and causally inert. This is a lot to swallow. And, again, it seems metaphysically supernatural; prima facie, believing in abstract objects seems to be like believing in ghosts or genies. We seem to have good reason *not* to believe in such things. We seem to have good reason to endorse a materialistic worldview according to which everything is physical. And so we seem to have good reason not to believe in abstract objects.

I don't know whether these remarks count as an *argument*. If not, and if you want an argument against platonism, you can use the widely discussed *epistemological* argument (developed by Benacerraf [1973] and Field [1989]). Here's a very simple version of this argument:

> Since abstract objects would exist outside of space and time (if they existed), and since we humans exist entirely within space and time, we could never acquire any knowledge of abstract objects. But platonism implies that mathematical knowledge *is* knowledge of abstract objects, and so platonism is incompatible with the fact that we humans *do have* mathematical knowledge.

There's a lot to say about whether this argument is good – that is, whether it succeeds in refuting platonism and motivating anti-realism[3] – but I won't say any more about this here because my aim in this Element is not to provide a positive argument for anti-realism. My aim is rather to defend anti-realism against the objections to that view.

2.3 Three Versions of Mathematical Anti-Realism

We can define mathematical anti-realism as just the negation of mathematical realism. So anti-realism is the view that it's not the case that our mathematical theories provide true descriptions of really existing mathematical objects. More roughly, but also more simply, anti-realism is the view that there are no such things as mathematical objects like numbers and sets and so on.[4]

There are numerous versions of anti-realism, and we can get a handle on these views by thinking about the argument for realism that I gave in Section 2.2.2 (i.e., the argument in [1]–[4]). That argument contains three premises – [1], [2], and [3] – and anti-realists have to reject one of these premises (because, together, they entail realism). And what we'll now see is that each of these three strategies of response leads to a different version of anti-realism. If we reject [1], we're led to *paraphrase nominalism*; if we reject [2], we're led to *deflationary-truth nominalism*; and if we reject [3], we're led to *error theory*. I will now articulate these three views.

2.3.1 Paraphrase Nominalism and the Rejection of Premise [1]

Paraphrase nominalism is the view that ordinary mathematical sentences should not be read at face value (and, in particular, that these sentences should not be read as making claims about objects). So, for example, '3 is prime' should not be read as being of the form '*Fa*' (and it should not be read as making a claim about the number 3); and 'There are infinitely many prime numbers' should not be read as asserting the actual existence of infinitely many objects; and so on.

There are a few different versions of paraphrase nominalism. Perhaps the most famous is *if-thenism*, which says that, for instance, '3 is prime' is best interpreted as expressing a conditional claim, such as 'If the entire series of natural numbers had existed, then it would have been the case that 3 was prime,' or 'Necessarily, if the entire series of natural numbers exists, then 3 is prime.' Versions of if-thenism have been developed by Putnam (1967, 1983), Horgan

---

[3] My own view is that the epistemological argument *isn't* good. See Footnote 8 for more on this.
[4] On some ways of categorizing views, certain kinds of *agnostics* (about the existence of mathematical objects) could count as anti-realists. But I won't worry about this here.

(1984), Hellman (1989), Dorr (2008), and Yablo (2017); moreover, a precursor to this view was endorsed by the early Hilbert (see Hilbert 1959 and his letters to Frege in Frege 1980). Finally, other versions of paraphrase nominalism have been endorsed by Wittgenstein (1956), Chihara (1990), Hofweber (2005), Rayo (2008, 2013), and Moltmann (2013).

The central idea behind most versions of paraphrase nominalism is that the non-face-value reading of mathematical sentences enables us to say that these sentences are true without committing to the existence of mathematical objects. For instance, if '3 is prime' really expresses a conditional claim, as if-thenists claim – in particular, if '3 is prime' really says that if the natural numbers had existed then it would have been the case that 3 was prime – then that sentence is true regardless of whether there's any such thing as the number 3.

2.3.2 Mathematical Error Theory and the Rejection of Premise [3]

Mathematical error theory (or, for short, just *error theory*) is the view that (a) the platonistic interpretation of mathematical discourse is correct – that is, our mathematical sentences and theories do *purport* to be about abstract mathematical objects, as platonists suggest – but (b) there are no such things as abstract objects, and so (c) our mathematical theories are not true. Thus, the idea here is that sentences like '3 is prime' are false, or untrue, for the same reason that, for instance, 'The Easter Bunny has big ears' is false or untrue – because just as there's no such thing as the Easter Bunny, so too there's no such thing as the number 3.[5] Error-theoretic views have been defended by Field (1980, 1989), me (Balaguer 1996, 1998, 2009), and Leng (2010).[6]

You might think error theory is untenable because you might think we have good reasons to think that our mathematical theories are true. But as we'll see in Section 3, it's harder than you might think to argue for the claim that our mathematical theories are strictly and literally true.

2.3.3 Deflationary-Truth Nominalism and the Rejection of Premise [2]

Deflationary-truth nominalism is the view that (a) ordinary mathematical sentences like '3 is prime' should be read at face value (i.e., as being of the form '*Fa*') and as making claims about mathematical objects; and (b) there are no such things as mathematical objects; but (c) our mathematical sentences are

---

[5] You might think, with Strawson (1950), that if there's no such thing as 3, then '3 is prime' is *neither true nor false*; I prefer the view that '3 is prime' is false in this scenario, and I'll assume that error theorists endorse that view, but nothing important turns on this.

[6] Also, related views have been defended by Melia (2000), Rosen (2001), and Yablo (2002a, 2002b, 2005).

still true. Views of this kind have been endorsed by Azzouni (2004, 2010) and Bueno (2005, 2009).

Deflationary-truth nominalism might seem hard to grasp. You might wonder how a sentence of the form '*Fa*' could be true if the singular term '*a*' doesn't refer to anything. How, for instance, could it be right to say that 3 is prime – that the number 3 has the property of being prime – if there's literally no such thing as the number 3? Isn't that like saying that (a) Mars is red, and (b) Mars doesn't exist? Isn't this incoherent?

But, in fact, there's an easy way to make coherent sense of deflationary-truth nominalism. The key is to understand the view as an empirical hypothesis about the meaning of the ordinary-language word 'true' – or, if you'd rather, about the ordinary concept of truth. When deflationary-truth nominalists say that, for instance, '3 is prime' could be true even if there were no such thing as the number 3, they're making a claim about the ordinary concept of truth – that is, about the concept that's expressed by the ordinary-language word 'true'. More specifically, they're saying that that concept applies in certain situations that most of us – mathematical platonists and error theorists and just about everyone else – think it *doesn't* apply in. So while you might *disagree* with deflationary-truth nominalism, the view is not incoherent.

Before moving on, it's worth distinguishing deflationary-truth nominalism from *Meinongianism*. The two views are superficially similar because Meinongians also claim that '3 is prime' could be true even if 3 didn't exist. But the similarity is only superficial because Meinongianism is a *realist* view, not an anti-realist view. Meinongians think that (a) there *is* such a thing as the number 3, and (b) the sentence '3 is prime' provides a true description of the number 3, but (c) despite all of this, 3 doesn't *exist*. Claims (a) and (b) already commit Meinongians to realism. They just have a nonstandard view of what's required for an object – a *real* object, an object that *is* – to count as "existing." In contrast to this, deflationary-truth nominalists wouldn't say that there *is* such a thing as the number 3; on the contrary, they think that there's no such thing at all.[7]

2.4 Some Arguments against Paraphrase Nominalism and Deflationary-Truth Nominalism

In Section 3, I'm going to respond to some objections to error theory, and in the process, I'll be trying to show that however implausible error theory might seem at first blush, it turns out to be fairly plausible, and indeed, there are reasons to

---

[7] Meinongian views have been endorsed by Routley (1980), Priest (2003, 2005), and of course Meinong (1904).

think it's the best version of anti-realism. But before I get to that, I want to argue against paraphrase nominalism and deflationary-truth nominalism.

2.4.1 An Argument against Paraphrase Nominalism

One problem with paraphrase nominalist views is that they commit to empirical claims about the meanings of ordinary mathematical utterances that are extremely implausible. For instance, if-thenism implies that ordinary utterances of '3 is prime' make conditional claims – for example, that *if the natural numbers had existed, then 3 would have been prime.* But this just seems to get wrong what ordinary people and ordinary mathematicians actually mean when they utter sentences like this. Certain kinds of *philosophers* – namely, those who don't believe in abstract objects – might think it would be *nice* if '3 is prime' really meant that if the natural numbers had existed, then 3 would have been prime. For we could then say that these sentences are true without committing to the existence of abstract objects. But in point of actual fact, it seems that, in ordinary English, '3 is prime' just *doesn't* mean that if the natural numbers had existed, then 3 would have been prime. That's just not what ordinary speakers mean when they utter '3 is prime,' and that's not what this sentence means in ordinary English.

More generally, we seem to have good reason to interpret ordinary mathematical sentences at face value; in other words, we have good reason to accept premise [1] and, hence, to reject all versions of paraphrase nominalism. The argument I have in mind here is based on the following, very plausible, interpretive principle:

> [IP] In general, when we're interpreting people's utterances, we should interpret them at face value unless there's evidence that they have positive intentions to be speaking nonliterally.

So if Jane utters the sentence 'Brindisi is in the heel of Italy's boot,' it's very likely that she intends (at some level, perhaps unconsciously) to be speaking nonliterally. And so it's acceptable to interpret Jane as speaking nonliterally in this case. But it seems that when ordinary people and ordinary mathematicians utter sentences like '3 is prime,' they usually don't intend (consciously or unconsciously) to be speaking nonliterally. For example, they don't intend to be expressing conditional propositions. On the contrary, it seems that they intend to be speaking literally. And so, given how plausible [IP] is as an interpretive principle, it seems that we should interpret ordinary speakers of mathematical sentences as speaking literally. And if this is right, then paraphrase nominalism is false.

Paraphrase nominalists might respond to this by claiming that they're not committed to the claim that their paraphrases capture the real meanings of the actual mathematical utterances of ordinary people and ordinary mathematicians. They might claim that they're telling us what we *should* mean by our mathematical sentences – or something like that.

But if paraphrase nominalists say this, then their view will presumably collapse into a version of error theory. For if they interpret ordinary mathematical utterances at face value – as being about abstract objects like numbers and sets – and if they don't believe in such objects, then they'll presumably have to say that ordinary mathematical utterances aren't true. Paraphrase nominalism would thus become a version of error theory – a version that tells us what we should do about the fact that our *actual* mathematical theories aren't true.

2.4.2 Two Arguments against Deflationary-Truth Nominalism

We saw in Section 2.3.3 that deflationary-truth nominalists should be interpreted as making an empirical claim about the meaning of the word 'true' in ordinary English. But given this, one obvious problem with deflationary-truth nominalism is that their empirical claim just seems *false*. To bring this out, consider the following sentence:

[M] Mars doesn't exist at all, but it's red.

Here's an empirical hypothesis of my own: [M] will strike most competent speakers of English as incoherent, or contradictory, or some such thing. But deflationary-truth nominalists are committed to the claim that [M] isn't incoherent or contradictory; they're committed to the view that [M] could very well be true. But that just seems to get things wrong. Thus, in short, my claim is this: deflationary-truth nominalism is incompatible with the usage and intentions of ordinary speakers regarding the word 'true.' Thus, the deflationary-truth nominalist's hypothesis about the ordinary-language meaning of 'true' is empirically implausible. In other words, it seems that, in point of actual empirical fact, the ordinary concept of truth just doesn't apply to any '*Fa*' sentences that have non-referring singular terms.

This argument is very quick, and there are various ways in which deflationary-truth nominalists might respond. But I won't discuss this any further here because I think there's another, more important, problem with deflationary-truth nominalism. I think it can be argued that, in the present context, it simply doesn't *matter* whether deflationary-truth nominalists are right about the ordinary-language meaning of 'true.' For it seems to me that deflationary-truth nominalism doesn't actually give anti-realists a tenable way of responding to the argument for realism – that is, the argument in [1]–[4]. This is because realists can counter the deflationary-truth nominalist's denial of premise [2] by (a) defining two different kinds of truth – we can call them *deflationary truth* and *non-deflationary truth*, where the former can apply to sentences of the form '*Fa*' even if the singular term '*a*' doesn't refer to anything, and the latter can't apply in such cases – and then (b) restating their argument in terms of the concept of non-deflationary truth. In other words, realists can replace all instances of the word 'true' in [1]–[4] with the expression 'non-deflationarily true,' which they define by stipulation in a way that enables them to avoid the deflationary-truth maneuver. If realists do this, then premise [2] will be analytic, or true by definition, and so the anti-realist's only options will be to reject premise [1] or premise [3] – or, rather, the *new* premise [3], which says that mathematical sentences like '3 is prime' are non-deflationarily true.

If realists reformulate the argument in [1]–[4] in this way, then deflationary-truth nominalists will respond in the same way that error theorists do, namely, by rejecting the new premise [3] – that is, by denying that our mathematical theories are non-deflationarily true. Moreover, it's important to note that error theorists agree with deflationary-truth nominalists that our mathematical theories *are deflationarily true* – and that this doesn't commit us to the existence of mathematical objects. So error theorists and deflationary-truth nominalists agree that (a) our mathematical theories *are* deflationarily true, and (b) these theories are *not* non-deflationarily true.

The difference between the two views is that deflationary-truth nominalism involves a commitment to the following empirical hypothesis:

> *Controversial Empirical Hypothesis (or, for short, CEH)*: Deflationary truth is *real* truth; in other words, the ordinary English word 'true' expresses the concept of deflationary truth, rather than the concept of non-deflationary truth.

Given this, deflationary-truth nominalism implies (and error theory doesn't imply) that our mathematical theories are *true*.

I want to make three points about this. First, it's worth noting that deflationary-truth nominalists more or less *have* to endorse CEH. You might have thought that they didn't; you might have thought that they could claim merely that we *should* use the word 'true' to express *deflationary truth* – or something like that. But if deflationary-truth nominalists say this, then their view will collapse into a version of error theory; for they'll have to say that, on the *ordinary* meaning of 'true,' our mathematical theories *aren't true*. Thus, if deflationary-truth nominalists want to avoid the result that they're just error theorists of a certain kind, they need to endorse CEH.

Second, given that the difference between deflationary-truth nominalism and error theory boils down to the former's commitment to CEH, it seems that the difference is *unimportant*. This is because it's a *merely verbal* difference – it's just about what the word 'true' happens to mean in ordinary English – and, surely, this isn't important. No sensible person thinks that the question of whether we ought to endorse the existence of mathematical objects depends on whether ordinary folk happen to use the word 'true' to express the concept of deflationary truth or the concept of non-deflationary truth.

Third, while deflationary-truth nominalists endorse CEH, on some ways of setting things up, their view will still collapse into a version of error theory. To see why, notice first that everyone involved in this debate – not just error theorists and deflationary-truth nominalists, but *realists* as well – agrees that (a) our mathematical theories are deflationarily true, and (b) this doesn't entail that numbers exist. Thus, to repeat a point I made earlier in this section, when realists formulate their argument (i.e., the argument in [1]–[4]), they'll be careful to do it in terms of non-deflationary truth, rather than deflationary truth. Now, you might think that realists should formulate their argument in terms of *truth* – that is, *ordinary* truth – and that they should claim that ordinary truth is non-deflationary truth. But realists don't need to care about this issue at all. If they like, they can say this:

> We don't care what the word 'true' happens to mean in ordinary English. Our claim is that our mathematical theories are non-deflationarily true, and we think we've got good arguments for the claim that they're non-deflationarily true – regardless of whether the ordinary-language word 'true' expresses the concept of non-deflationary truth.

Moreover, error theorists can say something very similar. In particular, they can say this:

> We also don't care what the word 'true' means in ordinary English. We agree with deflationary-truth nominalists that our mathematical theories are deflationarily true – and that this doesn't entail that mathematical objects exist – but this is irrelevant because realists agree with this as well. Our claim – the claim we make to respond to the realist's argument – is that our mathematical theories *aren't non-deflationarily true*.

So the point here is this: If error theorists define their view in terms of non-deflationary truth – in particular, as the view that our mathematical theories aren't non-deflationarily true – then deflationary-truth nominalism will collapse into a version of error theory, *despite the fact that it involves a commitment to CEH*.

In sum, then, we can say this: (i) on some ways of setting things up, deflationary-truth nominalism is just a version of error theory; and (ii) even if we set things up so that deflationary-truth nominalism *isn't* just a version of error theory, the difference between the two views isn't important (because it's merely verbal); and (iii) deflationary-truth nominalism is probably just *false* (because CEH is probably false).

In what follows, I won't continue to talk about deflationary truth and non-deflationary truth. I'll just use the term 'true.' But when I do this, I'll be talking about non-deflationary truth. In other words, I'll be assuming that premise [2] is true – that is, that a sentence of the form '*Fa*' can't be true unless the singular term '*a*' refers to something. So, for example, I'll be assuming that if there's no such thing as the number 3, then '3 is prime' is not true.

2.5 Error Theory Takes Center Stage

If the arguments that I've given here against paraphrase nominalism and deflationary-truth nominalism are right, then the only version of anti-realism left standing is error theory. But you might think there are good arguments against error theory as well. That's what Section 3 will be about; I'll consider several arguments against error theory – or, what comes to the same thing, several arguments for the truth of our mathematical theories – and I'll argue that these arguments don't work, that error theorists can effectively respond to them.

3 Mathematical Error Theory Defended

3.1 Opening Remarks

In Section 2, I defined a version of mathematical anti-realism known as *mathematical error theory* – or, for short, just *error theory*. Error theory says that our mathematical sentences and theories – sentences like '3 is prime' and theories like Peano Arithmetic – are *not true*. This, error theorists tell us, is because (a) these sentences and theories make claims (or at least purport to make claims) about abstract objects, and (b) there are no such things as abstract objects. Now, prima facie, error theory might seem pretty implausible. But what *arguments* are there against this view? In other words, what arguments are there for thinking that our mathematical sentences and theories are strictly and literally true?

In this section, I will consider four different arguments against error theory. I'll focus mostly on one of these arguments – what I'll call *the objective-correctness argument* – and I'll explain in depth how error theorists can respond to that argument. After that, I'll quickly run through the remaining three arguments – namely, a Moorean argument, a Lewisian argument, and a Quine-Putnam indispensability argument – and I'll explain how error theorists can respond to those arguments as well. My aim will be to show that error theory is far more defensible and plausible than it might seem at first blush.

(There's also a fifth argument against error theory – what I'll call the *reliance-on-modality argument* – but I won't respond to that argument in this section; I'll respond to it in the second part of this Element instead.)

3.2 A FAPP-ist Account of Objective Mathematical Correctness

3.2.1 The Objective-Correctness Argument

The first argument against error theory – or for the truth of our mathematical theories – can be formulated as follows:

> *The Objective-Correctness Argument*: We need to endorse the truth of our mathematical theories in order to account for the obvious fact that mathematics is an objective, factual discipline. There's obviously a sense in which mathematical sentences like '3 is prime' are *right*, or *correct*, whereas sentences like '4 is prime' are *wrong*, or *incorrect*. Moreover, it doesn't seem that we're just making this up; it seems to be an *objective fact* that '3 is prime' is right and '4 is prime' is wrong. And it seems that the only way to account for this is to say that sentences like '3 is prime' are *true* and sentences like '4 is prime' are *false*. And so it seems that mathematical error theory isn't true.

3.2.2 FAPP-Truth

I think that error theorists can respond to the objective-correctness argument by arguing that (a) while sentences like '3 is prime' are *strictly speaking* false, there is nevertheless an objective sort of *correctness* that attaches to these sentences – or a sort of *for-all-practical-purposes truth* – and (b) we can use the fact that our mathematical sentences and theories are for-all-practical-purposes true in this way to account for the objectivity and factualness of mathematics and for the difference between sentences like '3 is prime' and sentences like '4 is prime.'

The first thing that error theorists need to do here is define the relevant sort of correctness, or for-all-practical-purposes truth. Roughly speaking, I think error theorists should say that a sentence is for-all-practical-purposes true – or, for short, *FAPP-true* – if and only if it would have been true if platonism had been true. To make this more precise, error theorists need to specify the kind of platonism that they're appealing to here. I think there are good reasons for error theorists to define FAPP-truth in terms of the following version of platonism:

> *Plenitudinous platonism*: There actually exists a plenitude of abstract objects (i.e., there actually exist abstract objects of all possible kinds).

I think there are good reasons – reasons that I've articulated elsewhere[8] – for thinking that plenitudinous platonism is the best version of platonism. Because of this, I think error theorists should define FAPP-truth as follows:

> A sentence is *for-all-practical-purposes true* – or, for short, *FAPP-true* – iff it would have been true if plenitudinous platonism had been true (i.e., if there had actually existed a plenitudinous realm of abstract objects).

If you like, you can think of FAPP-truth as being equivalent to *truth in the story of plenitudinous platonism*. But this isn't the official definition of FAPP-truth, and it's important to note that error theorists are not commit to the existence of *stories*.[9]

3.2.3 FAPP-ism

Given the above definition of FAPP-truth, error theorists can respond to the objective-correctness argument against their view by arguing for the following theory:

> *FAPP-ism*: (i) Regardless of whether our mathematical theories are strictly speaking true, they're FAPP-true; for example, '3 is prime' is FAPP-true. Moreover, (ii) FAPP-truth is a legitimate kind of objective correctness, worthy of the term 'for-all-practical-purposes truth.' Finally, (iii) the fact that our mathematical theories are FAPP-true can be used to account for the objectivity and factualness of mathematics and for the difference between sentences like '3 is prime' on the one hand and sentences like '4 is prime' on the other.

I'll use the term *'FAPP-ist error theory'* to denote the conjunction of FAPP-ism and error theory. It's important to note, however, that FAPP-ism is entirely independent of error theory; FAPP-ism could be true even if error theory is false – indeed, even if platonism is true. But the more important point here is that FAPP-ism is compatible with error theory, and if error theorists can argue that FAPP-ism is true – and, as we'll see in Section 3.2.5, I think they *can* – then they'll have a response to the objective-correctness argument against their view.

---

[8] Most notably, I've argued (Balaguer 1995, 1998, 2016) that platonists can provide an adequate response to Benacerraf's (1973) challenge – that is, they can provide an adequate explanation of how we humans could acquire knowledge of abstract objects, despite the fact that we exist wholly within space and time and have no information-gathering contact with those objects – if and only if they endorse plenitudinous platonism.

[9] Field (1980, 1989, 1998) defined a notion of *truth in the story of mathematics* that's similar to FAPP-truth. But on Field's view, the "story of mathematics" consists in *currently accepted mathematical axioms*, rather than plenitudinous platonism, and I've argued elsewhere (2009, 2021) that this was a mistake. Also, Field relied on a *follows-from* relation, instead of counterfactuals, and the arguments of Section 3.6 suggest that this was a mistake as well.

3.2.4 Proto-Mathematical Truths

It's important to notice that according to FAPP-ist error theorists, there are counterfactual truths lurking right behind our mathematical theories. For according to this view, to say that, for instance, '3 is prime' is FAPP-true is equivalent to saying that the following counterfactual is *strictly and literally true*:

> [CF] If there had actually existed a plenitudinous realm of abstract objects, then it would have been the case that 3 was prime.

According to FAPP-ist error theorists, counterfactuals like [CF] are the truths that are, so to speak, *behind* our mathematical theories. Given this, we can think of these sentences as *proto-mathematical truths*.

(Note, however, that FAPP-ist error theorists do *not* think that [CF] captures the *real content* of '3 is prime,' or what that sentence *really says*. If they thought that, they wouldn't be error theorists; they would be paraphrase nominalists, in particular, if-thenists.)

I'll also speak sometimes of proto-mathematical *facts*; these are the counterfactual facts that are expressed by sentences like [CF]. It's important to note, however, that my talk here of "facts" should be taken with a grain of salt. For I take counterfactual truths to be *modal* truths of a certain kind, and as we'll see in Section 8, while I think there are modal *truths*, I also think that these truths don't require anything of reality – they don't require reality to be some specific way – and so I don't think that by taking counterfactuals like [CF] to be *true*, error theorists are committed to the existence of reified counterfactual facts, or reified proto-mathematical facts. I'll have much more to say about these issues in Section 8.

3.2.5 The Argument for FAPP-ism

I'll argue in this subsection that FAPP-ism is true and that this gives error theorists a response to the objective-correctness argument against their view. FAPP-ism, recall, has three parts – (i), (ii), and (iii) – so I need to argue for all three of these parts.

Part (i) of FAPP-ism says that even if there are no such things as mathematical objects, so that our mathematical theories aren't strictly true, these theories are still FAPP-true. To argue for this, I need to argue that (a) sentences like '3 is prime' are FAPP-true, and (b) this doesn't require the existence of mathematical objects. But to say that sentences like '3 is prime' are FAPP-true is equivalent to saying that counterfactuals like [CF] are true. Thus, what I need to argue here is that (a) counterfactuals like [CF] are true, and (b) this doesn't require the existence of mathematical objects.

The full argument for this will emerge in Section 8. I'll argue there that various kinds of modal claims – including counterfactuals like [CF] – are true, and that this doesn't commit us to the claim that mathematical objects exist, or indeed, to any other claims about the nature of reality. But for now, I just want to point out that, *intuitively*, counterfactuals like [CF] seem to be true regardless of whether mathematical objects exist. Here's a little argument for the truth of [CF] that doesn't rely on the claim that mathematical objects exist:

> [CF] is true – indeed, it's *analytic* – because it's antecedent analytically entails its consequent. The antecedent of [CF] says that plenitudinous platonism is true. That view entails that there are abstract objects of all possible kinds, and so it entails that there are abstract objects *of the kinds that our mathematical theories are about* (I'm assuming here that our mathematical theories are consistent and, hence, that there *could* be objects of the kinds that they're about). Thus, plenitudinous platonism entails that the *natural numbers* exist. But the claim that the natural numbers exist entails that 3 is prime – and that's just the consequent of [CF]. So, again, the antecedent of [CF] entails its consequent.

You might worry that abstract objects will come in the back door here – because you might think that we need to endorse the existence of abstract objects (in particular, possible worlds) to account for the truth of *any* modal claim. That's the worry that I'll be addressing in the second half of this Element. For now, though, I'm just pointing out that abstract objects don't seem to be coming in the *front* door here; in particular, the truth of [CF] doesn't seem to require the existence of the number 3.

Part (ii) of FAPP-ism says that FAPP-truth is a legitimate kind of objective correctness, worthy of the term 'for-all-practical-purposes truth.' Part of the argument for this will emerge in Section 8. For (a) to say that sentences like '3 is prime' are FAPP-true is to say that counterfactuals like [CF] are true; and (b) I'll argue in Section 8 that counterfactuals like [CF] are *objectively* true. (Also, I just argued that [CF]'s antecedent *entails* its consequent, and if that's true, then [CF] is presumably *objectively* true.)

But there's another point worth bringing out here. The mathematical sentences that come out FAPP-true on the error theoretic view – and, indeed, that *are* FAPP-true – are precisely the sentences that come out true on the (plenitudinous) platonist view. In other words, (plenitudinous) platonists and FAPP-ist error theorists divide the mathematical sentences into "good" ones and "bad" ones in an extensionally equivalent way. For instance, '3 is prime' is FAPP-true, and '4 is prime' isn't. And so on. (In case you're wondering why '4 is prime' isn't FAPP-true, the reason is that even if the natural numbers existed, it wouldn't be the case that 4 was prime.)

So (a) it's an objective fact which mathematical sentences are FAPP-true, and (b) FAPP-truth applies to the exact set of sentences that platonists (and, indeed, just about all of us) think are true. I think that this is enough to give us the result that FAPP-truth is a legitimate kind of objective *correctness*, worthy of the term 'for-all-practical-purposes truth.' And so I think that part (ii) of FAPP-ism is true.

Moreover, I think that if parts (i) and (ii) are both true – if our mathematical sentences and theories are FAPP-true, and if this is a legitimate kind of objective correctness – then this gives FAPP-ist error theorists a way to account for (a) the fact that mathematics is an objective, factual discipline, and (b) the difference between sentences like '3 is prime' and sentences like '4 is prime.' But that's just what part (iii) of FAPP-ism says. And so if I'm right that parts (i) and (ii) of FAPP-ism are true, then part (iii) is true as well. And since FAPP-ism contains only three parts, it follows that FAPP-ism is true. Moreover, if FAPP-ism is true, then it clearly gives error theorists a response to the objective-correctness argument against their view – that is, it gives them a way to account for the objective correctness of mathematics and for the difference between sentences like '3 is prime' and sentences like '4 is prime'.

This gives me an argument for what I wanted to establish in this subsection. But I want to drive all of this home by arguing that the FAPP-ist view I've developed here is independently plausible as a view of the objective correctness of our mathematical theories. I'll do this by arguing that platonists should endorse a virtually identical view. This might be surprising. For surely platonists should say that the reason our mathematical theories are "correct" is that they're *true*, and the reason mathematics is an "objective, factual discipline" is that our mathematical theories provide accurate representations of objective mathematical facts – in particular, facts about abstract objects. But while platonists should indeed say this, I think they should also say something like the following:

> We (platonists) think that counterfactuals like [CF] are true. So we think that our mathematical theories are FAPP-true. Now, of course, we *also* think that these theories are *true* – because we think that mathematical objects like 3 actually *exist*. It's important to note, however, that this existence fact – the fact that mathematical objects actually exist – doesn't do any work in determining which mathematical sentences are the "correct" ones, or the "good" ones. For this is already completely determined by the proto-mathematical facts that FAPP-ist error theorists believe in – that is, the facts about which sentences are FAPP-true. Thus, perhaps surprisingly, the existence fact that platonists endorse isn't needed in order for there to be an objective sort of correctness that attaches to our mathematical theories, and

from a mathematical point of view (as opposed to a metaphysical point of view), the existence fact is completely uninteresting and unimportant.

Why should platonists endorse this view? Well, suppose that, as of right now, there are no mathematical objects (and that there never have been) but that tonight at midnight God is going to bring a plenitudinous realm of abstract mathematical objects into existence. On this supposition, it follows that, as of right now, sentences like '3 is prime' aren't true but that tomorrow they will be. Moreover, it's already determined *which* mathematical sentences are going to become true. This is determined by the proto-mathematical facts that already obtain today. To put the point differently, as of right now (without there being any mathematical objects), we can say that (a) the mathematical sentences are already separated into the "good" ones and the "bad" ones, and (b) when the mathematical realm pops into existence at midnight, there will be *no change* in the membership of these two sets (i.e., the "good" set and the "bad" set). All that will happen is that the "good" sentences will go from being FAPP-true to being true (and note that even after they become true, they'll still be FAPP-true as well).

So it seems that even if platonists are right that there exists a plenitude of abstract objects, that existence fact doesn't do anything to determine *which* mathematical sentences are the good ones, or the correct ones. Now, of course, if abstract objects exist, then they make it the case that the good/correct sentences are *true*, instead of just FAPP-true; but the existence of abstract objects doesn't do anything to determine which mathematical sentences are the *good* ones.

You might respond here by saying something like this: "You're only getting this result because you're assuming that if platonism is true, then plenitudinous platonism is true (i.e., that if abstract objects exist at all, then there's a plenitude of abstract objects). Given this assumption, it is of course true that the platonistic existence facts don't do anything to determine which mathematical sentences are good and which ones are bad. But if we drop this assumption, then the existence facts will play an important role in determining which mathematical sentences are good and which ones aren't."

But I think this is just false; in this scenario, the platonistic facts would play a role in determining which mathematical sentences were *true*, but they still wouldn't play any role in determining which ones were *good*. Suppose that at midnight, God created the natural numbers but not the real numbers. Then, for instance, '3 is positive' would be true and '3.5 is positive' would be false; but there wouldn't be any interesting sense in which the former was good and the latter was bad. '3.5 is positive' would still be FAPP-true, and it would still be "good" in all the ways that really matter. The right thing to say in this scenario would be that since God created only some of the possible abstract objects, only some of the good mathematical sentences became true.

So it seems to me that all of us – even platonists – should endorse something like the FAPP-ist view of the objective correctness of our mathematical theories. And this gives us a powerful argument for the claim that FAPP-ism is true and that error theorists can use it to respond the objective-correctness argument against their view.

3.3 Objections and Responses

In this section, I'll provide responses to three different worries about FAPP-ist error theory.

3.3.1 Intended Parts of the Mathematical Realm

Consider the following objection to plenitudinous platonism and FAPP-ist error theory:

> There are pairs of mathematical theories – for example, Zermelo–Frankel set theory plus the continuum hypothesis (ZF+CH) and Zermelo–Frankel set theory plus the negation of the continuum hypothesis (ZF+~CH) – such that (a) both of the theories are internally consistent, but (b) they're inconsistent with each other. But this creates a problem for plenitudinous platonism and FAPP-ist error theory. For since ZF+CH and ZF+~CH are both internally consistent, it seems to follow that they're both *possible* – that is, that both theories *could be true* and that the objects that they describe *could exist*. But if these objects *could* exist, then according to plenitudinous platonism, they *do* exist. But if both of these domains of objects exist – that is, if the objects described by ZF+CH exist, and the objects described by ZF+~CH also exist – then it seems that ZF+CH and ZF+~CH are *both true*. And so plenitudinous platonism seems to lead to contradiction; for it seems to imply that ZF+CH and ZF+~CH are both true. And if this is right, then FAPP-ist error theory is in trouble too – for it leads to the obviously undesirable result that ZF+CH and ZF+~CH are both FAPP-true.

Let me begin by explaining how I think plenitudinous platonists should respond to this objection, and then at the end, I'll explain how FAPP-ist error theorists can respond in an essentially equivalent way.

The problem with the objection to plenitudinous platonism is that that view does *not* entail that ZF+CH and ZF+~CH are both true. Rather, it entails that they both *accurately describe collections of abstract objects*, or parts of the mathematical realm. But as I've argued elsewhere (1998, 2009), plenitudinous platonists should not say that every purely mathematical theory that accurately describes a collection of abstract objects is true. Rather, they should define mathematical truth in terms of accurately describing the *intended* objects – or in terms of truth in the *intended* parts of the mathematical realm. More precisely, I argued in my (2009) that plenitudinous platonists should endorse the following view of mathematical truth:

> [T] A pure mathematical sentence S is *true* if and only if it's true in all the parts of the mathematical realm that count as intended in the given branch of mathematics (and there is at least one such part of the mathematical realm); and S is *false* if and only if it's false in all such parts of the mathematical realm (or there is no such part of the mathematical realm[10]); and if S is true in some intended parts of the mathematical realm and false in others, then there's no fact of the matter whether S is true or false.[11]

So while plenitudinous platonism entails that all internally consistent purely mathematical theories accurately describe parts of the mathematical realm, it does *not* entail that all such theories are true. Consider, for example, the sentence '16 doesn't have a successor.' This sentence is internally consistent, and so it follows from plenitudinous platonism that it accurately describes some mathematical structure. But it *doesn't* accurately describe the *natural-number* structure, and so (if we interpret this sentence according to the rules of ordinary English) it's *false*. And if you uttered this sentence intending to say something about the natural numbers (and if you were speaking English), then your utterance would be false. And if plenitudinous platonists endorse [T], as I think they should, then they can say that utterances like this are false. So, again, plenitudinous platonism does not entail that all purely mathematical theories that are internally consistent are true. In particular, it doesn't entail that ZF+CH is true, and it doesn't entail that ZF+~CH is true. And so it obviously doesn't entail that they're *both* true. And so the objection to plenitudinous platonism fails.

But this means that the objection to FAPP-ist error theory fails as well. For if plenitudinous platonism doesn't entail that either ZF+CH or ZF+~CH is true, then FAPP-ist error theory doesn't entail that either of them is FAPP-true. (If I'm right that plenitudinous platonists should define truth in the above

---

[10] We actually don't need this parenthetical remark because if there's no such part of the mathematical realm, then the claim that S is false in all such parts will be vacuously true.

[11] If plenitudinous platonists endorse [T], then they'll have to say that there could be bivalence failures in mathematics. Suppose, for example, that our full conception of the universe of sets isn't perfectly precise, and suppose in particular that ZF+CH and ZF+~CH are both perfectly consistent with our full conception of the universe of sets. Given this, if plenitudinous platonism and [T] are both true, then there's no fact of the matter whether CH is true or false. I've argued elsewhere (Balaguer 2009) that this is exactly what we *should* say, if our concept of set is imprecise in the above way, but I can't get into this here.

way – in terms of truth in the intended parts of the mathematical realm – then FAPP-ist error theorists should define FAPP-truth in terms of what *would be* true in the intended parts of the mathematical realm, if there were a (plenitudinous) mathematical realm. But given this, FAPP-ist error theory does not imply that either ZF+CH or ZF+~CH is FAPP-true.)

3.3.2 Counterfactuals Involving Reference Failures

Recall that FAPP-ist error theorists think that counterfactuals like the following are true:

> [CF] If there had actually existed a plenitudinous realm of abstract objects, then it would have been the case that 3 was prime.

But you might wonder how error theorists can claim that [CF] is true given that, on their view, the singular term '3' doesn't refer to anything. I have two things to say in response to this worry. First, I think that on the right way of reading [CF], the claim that [CF] is true is perfectly compatible with the claim that '3' doesn't refer. For (a) if the antecedent of [CF] had been true, then '3' would have had a referent, and (b) that referent would have been prime, and so (c) if the antecedent of [CF] had been true, then its consequent would have been true as well. And this, it seems to me, is sufficient for the truth of [CF].

Second, even if I'm wrong about how we ought to read [CF] – even if the truth of [CF] is incompatible with the claim that '3' doesn't refer – it wouldn't undermine my argument in any important way. For in this scenario, error theorists could just switch from relying on counterfactuals like [CF] to relying on counterfactuals like the following:

> [**] If there had been a plenitudinous mathematical realm, and if everything else (including our linguistic intentions) remained the same, then '3 is prime' sentence tokens (literally intended and literally interpreted) would have been true.

So error theorists don't really need to rely on counterfactuals like [CF]. But in what follows, I'll assume that the truth of [CF] is compatible with the claim that '3' doesn't refer, and so I'll be working with the idea that error theorists are committed to [CF]-type counterfactuals, not [**]-type counterfactuals.

3.3.3 Counterpossibles

Consider the following objection to FAPP-ist error theory:

> Error theorists should say not just that abstract objects *don't* exist but that they *couldn't* exist – and so FAPP-ist error theorists should say that counterfactuals like

[CF] are actually *counterpossibles*. But you might think this is problematic because you might think counterpossibles are all vacuously true (e.g., Williamson (2007) argues for this vacuist view).

I have two responses to this. First, error theorists (and other anti-realists) don't have to say that the existence of abstract objects is impossible, and indeed, I (and others) have argued elsewhere – see, for example, Field (1989), Hellman (1989), and (Balaguer 1998, 2021) – that the best versions of anti-realism are contingentist views that say that the existence of abstract objects is possible. Second, I just don't think that the vacuist view of counterpossibles is right. That view is badly counterintuitive, and it's at odds with the fact that we all use counterpossible reasoning all the time. I think that nowadays most philosophers endorse the non-vacuist view that at least some counterpossibles are non-vacuously true and false. In any event, there are lots of papers that develop ways to understand counterpossibles in non-vacuous ways; see, for example, Mares and Fuhrmann (1995), Nolan (1997), Brogaard and Salerno (2013), Bjerring (2014), and Bernstein (2016). Also, for an argument against Williamson's vacuist view, see Berto, French, Priest, and Ripley (2018).

3.4 Other Arguments against Error Theory

So far in this section, I've explained how error theorists can respond to the objective-correctness argument against their view. In this section, I'll provide quick responses to three more arguments against error theory.

3.4.1 The Quine-Putnam Argument

Consider the following argument for the truth of our mathematical theories – and, hence, against mathematical error theory:

> *The Quine-Putnam Argument*: We need to acknowledge that our mathematical theories are true because (a) they're embedded (or ineliminably embedded) in our scientific theories, and (b) our scientific theories are true.[12]

I think error theorists can respond to this argument by saying something like the following:

> If there are any such things as abstract objects, then they're causally inert. But given this, it follows that the truth of our empirical theories depends on two sets of facts that hold or don't hold independently of one another. One of these sets of facts is purely platonistic and mathematical, and the other is purely

---

[12] For articulations of this argument, see Quine (1961a, 1961b), Putnam (1971), Resnik (1997), Colyvan (2001), and Baker (2005, 2009).

physical and anti-platonistic.[13] Since these two sets of facts hold or don't hold independently of one another, we can maintain that (a) there does obtain a set of purely physical facts of the sort required here (i.e., the sort needed to make our empirical theories true), but (b) there doesn't obtain a set of purely platonistic facts of the sort required for the truth of our empirical theories (because there are no such things as abstract objects). Therefore, mathematical error theory is consistent with an essentially realistic view of empirical science because we can maintain that even if there are no such things as mathematical objects and, hence, our empirical theories aren't strictly true, these theories still paint an essentially accurate picture of the physical world because the physical world is just the way it needs to be for our empirical theories to be true. In other words, we can maintain that the physical world holds up *its end* of the empirical-science bargain. Here's another way to put all of this: we can say that while our empirical theories aren't strictly true, they're still correct in an important sense of the term because they're FAPP-true – that is, they're such that they would have been true if there had been a plenitudinous realm of abstract objects. The reason that we (error theorists) can endorse this line is that abstract objects would (if they existed) be causally inert; because of this, it wouldn't make any difference to the physical world if the whole plenitude of abstract objects suddenly popped into existence. This is why we can say of our empirical theories that they're FAPP-true (i.e., that they would have been true if there had been a plenitudinous realm of abstract objects). And so, in sum, error theorists can endorse the very same view of the correctness of our empirical theories that they endorse of the correctness of our mathematical theories.

I think this gives error theorists an adequate response to the Quine-Putnam argument. But one might press error theorists here by asking them why our empirical theories make reference to mathematical objects in the first place, given that those objects don't really exist. Why is this *helpful*? After all, it's not helpful in physics to refer to the Easter Bunny. So why is it helpful to refer to numbers?

But there's an obvious way for error theorists to respond to this question. They can say that mathematics functions in empirical science as a descriptive aid; more precisely, it gives us an easy way to make certain kinds of claims about the physical world. For instance, by using singular terms that refer (or *purport* to refer) to real numbers, we give ourselves an easy way to describe the temperature states of physical systems. In essence, the numerals serve as *names* of the possible temperature states. Instead of using names like 'Fred' and 'Barney' to refer to these states, we use names like '32 degrees Fahrenheit'; and this is very convenient because the possible temperature states are lined up in

---

[13] It doesn't follow from what I'm saying here that we can always separate out the content of mixed sentences – that is, sentences that refer to (or quantify over) abstract and concrete objects.

the same way that the real numbers are lined up (or would be lined up, if they existed).

This theory of the role that mathematics plays in empirical science also explains why it wouldn't matter to our empirical scientific endeavors if mathematical objects didn't actually exist so that our mathematical theories weren't strictly true. The reason this wouldn't undermine our scientific endeavors is that mathematics can do what it's supposed to do in empirical science – that is, it can succeed in its role as a descriptive aid – even if it isn't true. For instance, even if there are no such things as real numbers, it's still helpful to use real-number expressions to talk about temperature states. Indeed, it's easy to see that the question of whether real numbers actually exist is totally irrelevant to the usefulness of real-number expressions to temperature talk. If I tell you that it's 30 degrees Fahrenheit outside, I succeed in communicating something to you about the air outside, even if what I said isn't strictly true because the number 30 doesn't really exist. This, in a nutshell, is because (a) my claim is FAPP-true (assuming that the air outside is, in fact, the right temperature – that is, the temperature picked out by the expression '30 degrees Fahrenheit'); and (b) since numbers would be causally inert if they existed, it just doesn't matter to the state of the air outside whether numbers actually exist. It's not as if we think that the number 30 is somehow making the air outside be the temperature that it is. That number could pop in and out of existence, and nothing about the air would change. The sentence 'It's 30 degrees outside' would flip back and forth between being true and being false, but it would remain FAPP-true through all of this, and we wouldn't notice the flip-flopping, and indeed, it wouldn't matter to us at all. In short, since we're essentially just using the expression '30 degrees' as the name of a certain temperature state, it follows that the sentence 'It's 30 degrees outside' would have the exact same amount of usefulness to us regardless of whether numbers existed and regardless of whether this sentence was literally true.

(This is all very quick; I have developed this response to the Quine-Putnam argument in much more depth elsewhere [Balaguer 1996, 1998].[14])

3.4.2 Mooreanism

You might try to motivate the idea that our mathematical theories are true by claiming that sentences like '2 + 2 = 4' and '3 is prime' have *Moorean* status – or that it's just *obvious* that these sentences are true, or some such thing. But this won't do. The puzzle about what view to endorse in the philosophy of

---

[14] For a different response to the Quine-Putnam argument – one that requires error theorists to *nominalize* our mathematical theories – see Field (1980, 1989).

mathematics – whether we should endorse platonism or error theory or some other view – is generated by inconsistencies between things that seem obvious to us. In particular, it seems that we have to abandon one of the following three obvious-seeming claims: (i) '3 is prime' is true, (ii) '3 is prime' is a claim about the number 3, and it can be true only if that number exists, and (iii) there's no such thing as platonic heaven. We can't make any progress here by claiming that (i) is obvious, or that it has Moorean status, because of course, we could just as easily claim that (ii) and (iii) are obvious and that they have Moorean status. To solve this puzzle, we have to figure out *which* of these apparently obvious claims to reject. And the question we should be asking isn't which of them has "Moorean status", but which of them can be supported by good *arguments*.

Here's another way to put the point I'm making here. Platonists have given us very compelling arguments for the view that '3 is prime' makes a claim about an abstract object and that this sentence is true only if there really *are* abstract objects. But given this, and given that it's clearly *not* obvious that there are abstract objects, platonists can't very well claim that it *is* obvious that '3 is prime' is true. They can't have their cake and eat it to. You can't claim that a sentence S is true only if some entirely nonobvious proposition p is true and then turn around and claim that it's obvious that S is true!

Now, what platonists *can* say is that error theorists need to account for the *seeming obviousness* of sentences like '2 + 2 = 4' and '3 is prime.' But error theorists can clearly do this. The reason these sentences seem so obvious to us, according to error theorists, is that we don't usually think about the possibility of numbers not existing, and since this is the only way that these sentences could fail to be true, we essentially overlook the only possible scenario in which they're not true – and so they're truth seems almost inescapable to us.

3.4.3 Laughable Presumption

David Lewis (1991, p. 59) claimed that it would be laughably presumptuous to suggest that we should reject our mathematical theories for philosophical reasons, given the track records of these two disciplines. I responded to this argument at length in my (2009). The main point I made there is this: when error theorists say that our mathematical theories aren't true, they're not *criticizing* those theories; they're not saying that there's something *wrong* with those theories. Rather, they're criticizing the *philosophical* view that the mark of goodness in mathematics is truth. According to FAPP-ist error theorists, the mark of goodness in mathematics is FAPP-truth, not truth. Thus, since our mathematical theories are FAPP-true, they're *good*. And so, according to FAPP-ist error theorists, *there's nothing wrong with our mathematical theories*.

3.5 The Reliance-on-Modality Objection to Error Theory

The final objection to error theory that I want to discuss can be put in the following way:

> *The reliance-on-modality objection*: Mathematical error theorists are committed to the truth of counterfactuals like [CF] – that is, like 'If there had been a plenitudinous realm of abstract mathematical objects, then it would have been the case that 3 was prime.' But counterfactuals like this are *modal* claims, and there's no way to account for the truth of sentences like this without committing to the existence of abstract objects. More specifically, in order to account for the truth of [CF], we need to commit to the existence of possible worlds in which there are abstract objects – and this seems to commit us to the existence of abstract objects. But error theorists are committed to the claim that there are no such things as abstract objects. Therefore, error theory is an unstable view – it's supposed to give us a way to avoid committing to abstract objects, but it ends up committing to abstract objects in the end anyway.

The only tenable way for error theorists to respond to this argument, in my opinion, is to simply explain how counterfactuals like [CF] could be true even if there are no such things as abstract objects. The hunt for an explanation of this kind is what the second part of this Element is going to be about. But before I move on to the second part, I want to explain why mathematical anti-realists of the other two kinds – that is, paraphrase nominalists and deflationary-truth nominalists – face a similar problem. They too need to commit to the truth of certain kinds of modal claims, and so they also need an account of how these claims could be true, given that there are no such things as abstract objects. This point will emerge in Section 4.

3.6 Counterfactualism over Necessitarianism

I've suggested in this section that error theorists should define FAPP-truth counterfactually – in terms of what would be true if plenitudinous platonism were true – and that they should commit to the truth of counterfactuals like [CF]. But if error theorists wanted to avoid relying on counterfactuals, they could use the following alternative definition of FAPP-truth:

> *Alternative Definition of FAPP-truth*: A sentence S is FAPP-true iff necessarily, if there exists a plenitudinous realm of abstract objects, then S is true.

If error theorists used this definition, instead of the definition I proposed in Section 3.2.2, then they would be committed not to counterfactuals like [CF] but to necessitarian conditionals like

[N] Necessarily, if there exists a plenitudinous realm of abstract objects, then 3 is prime.

But I think there's a good reason for error theorists to (a) favor the counterfactual definition of FAPP-truth that I gave in Section 3.2.2 and (b) commit to the truth of counterfactuals like [CF] rather than necessitarian conditionals like [N]. The reason is that the counterfactual approach enables error theorists to endorse a uniform view of pure mathematical sentences like '3 is prime' and mixed sentences like 'The air outside is 32 degrees Fahrenheit (i.e., the air outside stands in the Fahrenheit-relation to the number 32).' We saw in Section 3.4.1 that error theorists who endorse the counterfactual approach – or, as we might call them, *counterfactual FAPP-ist error theorists* – can say the *same thing* about sentences of these two kinds. More generally, they can say the same thing about our empirical theories that they say about our pure mathematical theories, namely, that (a) our empirical theories are *FAPP-true* (i.e., they would have been true if plenitudinous platonism had been true) and (b) FAPP-truth (not truth) is the mark of goodness in empirical science. But error theorists who endorse the necessitarian approach – *necessitarian FAPP-ist error theorists* – can't endorse a uniform view here. For necessitarians can't plausibly commit to the sentence 'Necessarily, if there exists a plenitudinous realm of abstract objects, then the air outside is 32 degrees Fahrenheit.' Perhaps necessitarians could solve this problem by appealing instead to sentences like 'Necessarily, if there exists a plenitudinous realm of abstract objects (and if the actual world remains unchanged), then the air outside is 32 degrees Fahrenheit' – or something like that – but I think that error theorists are better off endorsing a counterfactualist view. (If I thought there were any good reasons for error theorists to favor the necessitarian approach over the counterfactual approach, then I might think it was worth trying to solve the above problem with the necessitarian view; but I don't think there are any good reasons for this.)

4 Paraphrase Nominalism and Deflationary-Truth Nominalism Revisited

4.1 Opening Remarks

We saw in Section 2 that there are three kinds of mathematical anti-realism, namely, paraphrase nominalism, deflationary-truth nominalism, and error theory. In this section, I'll argue that paraphrase nominalists and deflationary-truth nominalists encounter most of the same problems that I raised for error theorists in Section 3 – in particular, (i) the problem of accounting for the objectivity and factualness of our mathematical theories, and (ii) the problem of accounting for the usefulness of our mathematical theories in empirical science. I'll suggest that paraphrase nominalists and deflationary-truth nominalists can solve these problems in essentially the same way that error theorists solve them; but in order to do this, they need to commit to the truth of certain kinds of modal claims, just like error theorists do. And so I'll conclude that, just like error theorists, paraphrase nominalists and deflationary-truth nominalists encounter the worry that they can't account for the truth of the modal claims that they're committed to because these modal claims are incompatible with their mathematical anti-realism.

4.2 Problems for Paraphrase Nominalism

You might think that since paraphrase nominalists maintain that our mathematical theories are *true*, they won't have a hard time accounting for (a) the objective correctness of those theories or (b) the usefulness of those theories in empirical science. But one might reasonably doubt this. For one might think that since paraphrase nominalists deny that our mathematical theories make true claims about real objects – and since the best versions of paraphrase nominalism seem to imply that our mathematical theories are *analytic* (or something like analytic) – paraphrase nominalists can't maintain that our mathematical theories are true *in a substantive way*. In other words, one might think that while paraphrase nominalism implies that our mathematical theories are true, it implies that they're true in a rather hollow way. And so one might reasonably doubt that paraphrase nominalists can adequately account for the factualness of mathematics or the usefulness of mathematics in empirical science. And so it seems to me that paraphrase nominalists need to address these two points.

But I think that paraphrase nominalists – or at any rate, advocates of the best versions of paraphrase nominalism – can solve these two problems. In other words, I think they can account for (a) the objectivity and factualness of mathematics and (b) the usefulness of mathematics in empirical science. Consider, for example, the version of paraphrase nominalism that says that ordinary mathematical sentences really express counterfactual propositions; more specifically, according to the view I have in mind, sentences like '3 is prime' are equivalent to counterfactuals like

> [CF] If there had actually existed a plenitudinous realm of abstract objects, then it would have been the case that 3 was prime.

Let's call this view *counterfactual if-thenism*. The arguments of Section 3 already show how counterfactual if-thenists can account for the objectivity and factualness of mathematics and the usefulness of mathematics in empirical science. For (a) I argued in Section 3 that counterfactual FAPP-ist error theorists can account for these two things; and (b) counterfactual if-thenists can use essentially the same explanations that counterfactual FAPP-ist error theorists use because these two views are both based on the same underlying idea – namely, that counterfactuals like [CF] are objectively true. (The only significant difference between counterfactual FAPP-ist error theory and counterfactual if-thenism is that the latter says (and the former doesn't) that [CF] captures the *real content* of '3 is prime' – or what '3 is prime' *really says*.)

Similar remarks can be made about *necessitarian if-thenism*. (This is the view that ordinary mathematical sentences really express necessitarian conditionals; more specifically, on this view, sentences like '3 is prime' are equivalent to conditionals like

[N] Necessarily, if there exists a plenitudinous realm of abstract objects, then 3 is prime.)

It seems clear that necessitarian if-thenists (and necessitarian FAPP-ist error theorists) can account for the objectivity and factualness of mathematics in essentially the same way that counterfactual if-thenists and counterfactual FAPP-ist error theorists do – except that the necessitarians' theory will be based on the claim that necessitarian conditionals like [N] are objectively true, rather than the claim that counterfactuals like [CF] are objectively true.

But the point I really want to make here is this: All tenable versions of paraphrase nominalism rely on the idea that certain kinds of modal claims are true, and so advocates of these views are going to have to explain *how* the relevant modal claims could be true. This is transparently obvious in connection with counterfactual if-thenism and necessitarian if-thenism; for the former involves a commitment to counterfactuals, and the latter involves a commitment to necessitarian conditionals, and claims of both of these kinds are (obviously) modal claims.

I don't think there's any tenable way for paraphrase nominalists to avoid this. Suppose, for example, that paraphrase nominalists tried to endorse a material-conditional-style if-thenist view according to which '3 is prime' is equivalent to

[M1] If the entire series of natural numbers exists, then 3 is prime.

This view clearly won't give paraphrase nominalists what they need. For if the natural numbers don't *in fact* exist, as paraphrase nominalists claim, then advocates of this material-conditional if-thenist view will be committed to saying not just that sentences like [M1] are true, but also that sentences like the following are true:

[M2] If the entire series of natural numbers exists, then 4 is prime.

Indeed, material-conditional if-thenists have to say that *every* material conditional with that same antecedent is true, regardless of what its consequent says. And so if paraphrase nominalists claim that sentences like '3 is prime' are equivalent to sentences like [M1], then they won't be able to capture the fact that '3 is prime' is true and '4 is prime' is false.

More generally, it's hard to see how *any* paraphrase nominalist view that didn't rely on any modal claims (or something similar) could be tenable. One way to appreciate this is to remember that it's an important fact about mathematical practice that non-axiomatic arithmetical claims like '3 is prime' *follow from* the axioms of arithmetic. In other words, if the axioms of arithmetic are true, then it *must* be the case that 3 is prime. Or to put the point differently, if we assume that the axioms are true, then we can *prove* that 3 is prime. This is obviously a very important feature of mathematical practice, and it's hard to see how paraphrase nominalists could account for this without committing to modal claims, in particular, necessitarian claims.

You might think that paraphrase nominalists could do this by employing a notion of *entailment*, rather than a notion of necessity. But how are we to define entailment? One way to define it is to say that p *entails* q iff it's impossible for p-and-not-q to be true; but on this definition, entailment just *is* a modal notion. Alternatively, we could define entailment syntactically (in terms of *proofs*) or semantically (in *model-theoretic* terms); but both of these strategies will end up committing us to abstract objects (because proofs and models are both abstract objects). Finally, paraphrase nominalists could take entailment to be a *primitive*; but if they do that (and if the primitive notion in question does what the notion of entailment is supposed to do, and what anti-realists need it to do if they're going to account for all of the relevant facts about mathematical practice), then it's hard to see why this primitive notion of entailment wouldn't just *be* a modal notion (or close enough to a modal notion that the difference wouldn't matter for our purposes here[15]).

I won't say any more about this here. I'll just assume in what follows that any tenable version of paraphrase nominalism commits to the truth of modal claims.

---

[15] If paraphrase nominalists take 'entails' to be a primitive, they'll still need to say what makes entailment claims true, regardless of whether they characterize such claims as "modal" claims; and when they try to do this, they'll encounter essentially the same problems that we encounter in trying to account for the truth of sentences that involve primitive *modal* operators. So, again, the difference won't matter much for our purposes here.

4.3 Problems for Deflationary-Truth Nominalism

You might think that since deflationary-truth nominalists deflate the notion of truth, and since they claim that mathematics is true in a deflated way, they don't salvage a substantive kind of truth for mathematics, and so they can't account for the fact that mathematics is objectively correct or the fact that it's useful in empirical science.

I don't think this is right; I think that deflationary-truth nominalists can account for what they need to account for here. But I also think that in order to account for the relevant facts about mathematics – for example, that mathematics is an objective, factual discipline, that mathematics is useful in empirical science, that proof plays a central and important role in mathematical practice, and so on – deflationary-truth nominalists need to commit to the truth of modal claims of one kind or another. But I won't take the space to argue for this here because the arguments are very similar to the arguments that I've already run in connection with error theory and paraphrase nominalism – and because I think that, by now, the point is more or less obvious.

If I'm right about this – if, like error theorists and paraphrase nominalists, deflationary-truth nominalists need to appeal to modal claims in order to account for various facts about mathematical practice – then anti-realists of all three kinds need to explain how the modal claims in question could be true, given that there are no such things as abstract objects. For example, they need to explain how counterfactuals like [CF], or necessitarian conditionals like [N], could be true, given that there are no such things as abstract objects. Or perhaps better, anti-realists need to answer the following question:

> What *makes* the relevant modal claims true, given that there are no such things as abstract objects?

The second part of this Element is about this question. It's about whether anti-realists can answer this question and, if they can, *how* they can answer it.

MODAL NOTHINGISM

5 Modal Semantics and Modal Truthmaking

5.1 Opening Remarks

As we saw in Section 2, we can define mathematical anti-realism as just the negation of mathematical realism, where mathematical realism is the view that (a) there exist mathematical objects (e.g., numbers and sets), and (b) our mathematical theories provide true descriptions of these objects.

So *mathematical anti-realism* is the view that it's not the case that our mathematical theories provide true descriptions of really existing mathematical objects.

We also saw in Section 2 that the only tenable version of mathematical realism is *platonism*, where this is just the conjunction of realism and the claim that mathematical objects are *abstract* objects – that is, nonphysical, nonmental objects that aren't located anywhere (i.e., that don't exist in space or time) and are completely unextended and acausal. So one of the central claims of anti-realism is that there are no such things as abstract objects.

Finally, we found in Sections 3 and 4 that in order for anti-realists to respond to certain kinds of objections, and in order to provide an adequate account of mathematical practice, they need to commit to the truth of certain kinds of *modal* claims. Different anti-realists commit to the truth of different kinds of modal claims. The versions of anti-realism that we looked at most closely commit to the truth of counterfactuals like the following:

> [CF] If there had actually existed a plenitudinous realm of abstract objects, then it would have been the case that 3 was prime.

Other anti-realist views commit to other kinds of modal claims; for example, some anti-realist views commit to necessitarian conditionals like

> [N] Necessarily, if there exists a plenitudinous realm of abstract objects, then 3 is prime.

But while different kinds of anti-realists commit to different kinds of modal truths, they all need to commit to the truth of modal claims of one kind or another.

But there's a potential problem for anti-realists here. For (a) mathematical anti-realists don't believe in abstract objects, and (b) one might plausibly think that in order to account for the truth of modal claims, we need to posit the existence of abstract objects. So it's not clear that anti-realists can account for the truth of modal claims. And so in order to make their view plausible, anti-realists need to show that they *can* account for the truth of modal claims. In short, they need to explain how modal claims of the relevant kind could be true, even if there are no such things as abstract objects.

In this second part of this Element, I will discuss the question of whether mathematical anti-realists can provide the needed explanation here and, if they can, what that explanation looks like. I will eventually get around to discussing counterfactuals like [CF] and necessitarian conditionals like [N]; but it will simplify things considerably if we begin by focusing on simple possibility claims like the following:

[Possible] There could have been flying saucers.

There are two important and interrelated questions that we can ask about modal sentences like [Possible]. One is a *semantic* question that asks what these sentences *mean*, or what they *say*. The other is a *truthmaking* question that asks what it is about *reality* that *makes* modal sentences like [Possible] true.

In this section, I'll introduce these two questions, and I'll argue that mathematical anti-realists owe us an answer to the truthmaking question.

5.2 The Semantic Question

There are two mainstream analyses of ordinary modal sentences like [Possible]. In this section, I'll articulate these two views, and then at the end, I'll quickly mention a third view that one might endorse.

5.2.1 The Possible-Worlds Analysis of Ordinary Modal Discourse

Roughly speaking, according to the possible-worlds analysis of ordinary modal discourse, to say that something is *possible* is to say that there exists a possible world in which it's true; and to say that something is *necessary* is to say that it's true in *all* possible worlds. Thus, on this view, [Possible] is equivalent to the following sentence:

[PossibleWorld] There exists a possible world in which there are flying saucers.

When I say that, according to the possible-worlds analysis, [Possible] is *equivalent* to [PossibleWorld], what I mean is that, according to this view, these two sentences *say the same thing*. In other words, on this view, [Possible] already says that there *is* a possible world where there are flying saucers. And so, if we assume for the sake of argument that there aren't any flying saucers in the *actual* world (i.e., in *our* world), we get the result that, according to the possible-worlds analysis, [Possible] already implies that there are *other* possible worlds – that is, that there really exist *non-actual* possible worlds.[16]

5.2.2 The Primitivist Analysis of Ordinary Modal Discourse

According to *modal primitivism*, or *the primitivist analysis of ordinary modal discourse*, sentences like [Possible] involve primitive modal operators rather than quantification over possible worlds. To get a more precise statement of this

---

[16] This view has been endorsed by many philosophers, most notably, Lewis (1986).

view, let me introduce the terms 'possibly*' and 'necessarily*,' and let me stipulate that the former is a primitive sentential possibility operator and the latter is a sentential necessity operator that's defined in terms of the former in the usual way. Given this, we can say that according to the primitivist analysis of ordinary modal discourse, [Possible] is equivalent to the following sentence:

[Possible*] Possibly*, there are flying saucers.

Thus, on this view, [Possible] doesn't say that there's some other world where there *are* flying saucers; it just says that there *could have been* flying saucers; period.[17]

(It's important to note that on the primitivist view I've got in mind, 'possibly*' expresses the *broadest* kind of possibility. I'll say more in Section 7.2 about what the broadest kind of possibility *is*, but for now, we don't need to worry about this.)

One more thing about modal primitivism. In addition to 'possibly*' and 'necessarily*,' I'd like to introduce a new *counterfactual* operator – 'if it had been the case that . . ., then it would* have been the case that . . . ' – and I want to stipulate that, as I'm using the term 'modal primitivism,' that view says that the counterfactual operator of ordinary language is synonymous with this new counterfactual operator.

This raises the question of whether modal primitivists maintain that (i) the new counterfactual operator (i.e., ' . . . would* . . . ') is an extra *primitive* term, in addition to 'possibly*,' or (ii) ' . . . would* . . . ' can be defined in terms of 'possibly*' and 'necessarily*.' But I won't worry about this issue here. My own view is that view (i) is superior to view (ii), but I won't try to justify this claim here, and I'll assume that both of these views are available to modal primitivists.[18]

(If mathematical anti-realists endorse a necessitarian view – that is, if they commit to necessitarian conditionals like [N] rather than counterfactuals like [CF] – then they won't have to use ' . . . would* . . . ' at all, and so they won't have to worry about whether it can be defined in terms of 'possibly*' and 'necessarily*.' But as I pointed out in Section 3.6, I think anti-realists are better off committing to counterfactuals like [CF] than necessitarian conditionals like [N].)

---

[17] Primitivism has been endorsed by, for example, Forbes (1989), Shalkowski (1994), and Bueno and Shalkowski (2009).

[18] You might think we can define 'If it had been the case that P, then it would* have been the case that Q' by saying that it's equivalent to the following: 'Necessarily*, if P (and if everything else is as similar (or as "close") as possible* to the way that things actually are, given that P), then Q.' But (a) this requires us to rely on a notion of *similarity*; and (b) I have doubts about whether this definition is adequate; and (c) I don't think modal primitivists have any good reason to avoid saying that ' . . . would* . . . ' is an extra primitive.

5.2.3 Hybrid-Mess-ism

Here's a third view that we can endorse or ordinary modal discourse:

> *Hybrid-Mess-ism*: Ordinary modal discourse is a semantic mess. More spe-
> cifically, some ordinary modal claims (e.g., 'There are two ways the election
> could turn out') are best read as involving quantification over possible
> worlds, and other ordinary modal claims (e.g., 'There could have been flying
> saucers') are best read as involving primitive modal operators like 'pos-
> sible*.' All of these claims should just be read at *face value*. 'There are two
> ways the election could turn out' seems on its face to involve quantification
> over possible worlds – or what comes to the same thing, *ways the world could
> be* – and it really *does*. And 'There could have been flying saucers' *doesn't*
> seem to involve quantification over worlds – and it really doesn't.

I find this view quite plausible. One benefit of it is that we can always endorse
the most plausible interpretation of each sentence; so, for example, we don't
have to endorse an implausible primitivist reading of 'There are two ways the
election could turn out,' or an implausible possible-worlds reading of 'There
could have been flying saucers.' But I won't try to argue here that Hybrid-Mess-
ism is true.

In what follows, I will mostly focus on the primitivist and possible-worlds
analyses of ordinary modal discourse; but I will sometimes also refer to Hybrid-
Mess-ism.

5.3 The Truthmaking Question

Consider the following question:

> *The truthmaking question*: Assuming that modal sentences like [Possible] are
> true, what *makes* them true? In particular, what is it about *reality* that makes
> these sentences true?

To properly understand this question, let's forget about modal sentences for
a moment and think about ordinary sentences like

[Red] Mars is red.

It seems that this sentence is true and that there's something about reality that
makes it true. In particular, it seems that there's something about *Mars* that
makes it true – namely, its being red.

Some philosophers (e.g., Armstrong (1997)) think that every true sentence is
made true by a *truthmaker*. A truthmaker for a sentence S is an entity E whose
mere existence *necessitates* S; in other words, the idea here is that 'E exists'
entails S. Now, one thing to note here is that Mars itself is not a truthmaker for

[Red] – because Mars could exist without being red. So if [Red] has a truthmaker, it's presumably a *fact*, or a *state of affairs* – in particular, the fact (or state of affairs) of Mars being red.

But you might doubt that there are such things as reified facts, or states of affairs, that really exist out there in reality. If so, then [Red] presumably doesn't have a truthmaker. But despite this, we should still maintain that there's something about reality – and, in particular, about Mars – that makes [Red] true. We might put this by saying that [Red] is made true by Mars *and how Mars is* (in particular, by its being red). And you might think this generalizes; in particular, you might think the following principle is true:

> *All Truths are Made True by Reality (or for short, TMR):* For any true sentence S, there's something about reality (or about how things are in reality, or some such thing) that *makes S true*. Put differently, the idea here is that S is made true by (a) what exists and (b) how the existent things are.[19]

Prima facie, TMR seems extremely plausible. Indeed, it's hard to see what it could even mean to say that a sentence is true if there's nothing about reality that makes it true.[20]

So this is what generates the above truthmaking question about modal sentences like [Possible]. It seems that if sentences like [Possible] are true, then there must be something about reality that *makes* them true. But it's not clear *what exactly it is* about reality that makes [Possible] true. For even if you believe in reified facts – for example, even if you believe that *the fact that Mars is red* exists out there in reality – it's not at all obvious that there's a fact (out there in reality) that makes [Possible] true. Where would that fact – the fact that there could have been flying saucers – be *located*? Prima facie, facts of this kind don't seem to be located anywhere, and they don't seem to be *made* of anything. And so anyone who doesn't believe in abstract objects – for example, mathematical anti-realists – would likely be disinclined to believe in free-floating facts of this kind. And so there's a worry here about how mathematical anti-realists can account for the truth of ordinary modal claims.

I suppose you might think that there actually *are* flying saucers and that this is what makes [Possible] true. But let's assume for the sake of argument that there *aren't* any flying saucers (i.e., that there aren't any objects that satisfy the folk concept of a flying saucer). Given this, it's not at all clear what makes [Possible] true.

---

[19] Lewis (1992), Parsons (1999), and Dodd (2002) all reject the truthmaker thesis (i.e., the thesis that every true sentence has a truthmaker) in favor of a weaker claim along the lines of TMR.

[20] This is especially true if we remember that we're talking here about *non-deflationary* truth. See Sections 2.4.2 and 8.9 for more on this.

5.4 The Mathematical Anti-Realist's Predicament

It seems to me that what mathematical anti-realists need to do, primarily, is answer the truthmaking question. They need to explain how the modal sentences that they're committed to could be true, even if there are no such things as abstract objects. And to do that, it would seem, they need to answer the truthmaking question for these modal sentences. Now, it might seem that in order to answer the truthmaking question, they also need to answer the semantic question. I'm eventually going to argue, however, that this isn't right – that mathematical anti-realists can solve this problem with their view while maintaining a semantic neutrality (i.e., without committing to any specific view about how folk modal discourse should be interpreted). But we needn't worry about this just yet.

For now, what I want to do is simply explore the mathematical anti-realist's options, vis-à-vis the semantic question and the truthmaking question. In Section 6, I'll consider the question of whether mathematical anti-realists can endorse a possible-worlds view; and in Section 7, I'll consider whether they can endorse a primitivist view. What we're going to find is that mathematical anti-realists have very few viable options here. Indeed, it's going to seem that they don't have *any* viable options. But I'll then argue in Section 8 that there is a way out of this pickle for anti-realists.

6 Possible Worlds

6.1 Opening Remarks

The possible-worlds analysis of ordinary modal discourse brings with it an answer to the truthmaking question. In particular, it follows from the possible-worlds analysis that if ordinary modal claims are true, then they're made true by facts about (really existing) possible worlds.

Given this, it might seem that mathematical anti-realists can't endorse the possible-worlds analysis of ordinary modal discourse. But looks can be deceiving, and so I want to explore this question in the present section. There are three different strategies that mathematical anti-realists might pursue, if they endorse the possible-worlds analysis of ordinary modal discourse. First, they could try to claim that (a) modal claims are made true by facts about possible worlds, and (b) possible worlds are *not* abstract objects. Second, they could try to endorse a modal error theory – claiming that while our modal sentences purport to be about possible worlds, there are no such things as (non-actual) possible worlds, and so (most of) our modal sentences *aren't true*. Or, third, they could endorse a deflationary-truth view according to which our modal sentences are claims about possible worlds, and there are no such things as (non-actual) possible worlds, but despite this, these modal claims are still true.

I'll discuss the first strategy in Section 6.2, the second strategy in Section 6.3, and the third strategy in Section 6.4.

6.2 Realism about Possible Worlds

In broad brush strokes, there are two views about the nature of possible worlds. According to one view, possible worlds are abstract objects of some sort – properties, or sets of sentences or propositions, or some such thing.[21] Obviously, mathematical anti-realists can't endorse this view; more precisely, they can't say that there *are* such things as possible worlds and also say that they are abstract objects; for anti-realists are committed to saying that there are no such things as abstract objects.

The second view of possible worlds (roughly, the Lewisian (1986) view) is that non-actual possible worlds are just like the actual world in kind – they're just *different* worlds. On this view, the actual world isn't special in any objective, metaphysical way; it's just the world where we happen to be located. So the difference between the actual world and non-actual worlds is, on this view, analogous to the difference between Earth and Mars. Earth and Mars are objects of the *same kind* – in particular, they're both just planets – and Earth isn't special in any objective, metaphysical way; it's just the planet that we happen to live on.

According to this Lewisian view, possible worlds are *concrete* objects; roughly, they're spatiotemporal manifolds. Thus, if you endorsed this view, then you could account for the truth of modal claims like [Possible] (i.e., like 'There could have been flying saucers') without committing to the existence of abstract objects. For you could maintain that [Possible] is made true by the existence of non-actual (concrete) worlds where there are (concrete) flying saucers.

But the modal sentences that mathematical anti-realists are committed to aren't like [Possible]; as we've seen, anti-realists are committed to modal sentences like the following:

> [CF] If there had actually existed a plenitudinous realm of abstract objects, then it would have been the case that 3 was prime.

> [N] Necessarily, if there exists a plenitudinous realm of abstract objects, then 3 is prime.

Could mathematical anti-realists account for the truth of sentences like [CF] and [N], if they endorsed the possible-worlds analysis of ordinary modal discourse

---

[21] For articulations of this view, see, for example, Stalnaker (1976), Plantinga (1976), and Cameron (2009b).

and a Lewisian view of the nature of possible worlds? Well, for starters, let me note that while Lewis thought that possible worlds were concrete objects, he also believed in *abstract* objects – and, in particular, he believed in mathematical objects like numbers and sets. Now, on Lewis's specific version of this view, there's one platonic realm of abstract objects that serves as the platonic realm for all the possible worlds. But you could endorse a roughly Lewisian view of possible worlds – claiming that they're of the same kind as the actual world – and then go on to claim that (a) abstract objects are *worldbound* and (b) they exist in some worlds but not others, so that there are some platonist worlds and some anti-platonist worlds. More specifically, if you wanted to, you could claim that the actual world is an anti-platonist world (i.e., that there are no abstract objects in the actual world) but that there are *other* worlds where platonism is true – indeed, where plenitudinous platonism is true. And if you held this view, then you could say that (a) mathematical anti-realism is true (because there are no abstract objects in the *actual* world), and (b) modal sentences like [CF] and [N] are also true (because they're true claims about the whole space of possible worlds).

But I take it that no mathematical anti-realist would endorse this view. For this view commits us to saying that *there do exist abstract objects*. They don't exist *in the actual world*, on this view, but so what? They still exist *in reality*. The whole point of mathematical anti-realism is that it enables us to say that there are no abstract objects *at all*. And so, again, I take it that this weird Lewis-inspired version of mathematical anti-realism is a nonstarter.

And given this, I think we can say that there's just no stable way for mathematical anti-realists to (a) endorse the existence of possible worlds and (b) maintain that this enables them to account for the truth of modal claims like [CF] and [N].

6.3 Modal Error Theory

Consider the following view:

> *Modal Error Theory:* (a) The possible-worlds analysis of ordinary modal discourse is true (i.e., ordinary modal sentences are about – or at least *purport* to be about – possible worlds); but (b) there are no such things as non-actual possible worlds; and so (c) ordinary modal sentences like [Possible] are not true (or at any rate, they're not non-accidentally true[22]).[23]

---

[22] Some modal sentences come out *accidentally* true on this view. Consider, for example, 'Necessarily, there are dogs' and 'Possibly, there are dogs.' If there are no non-actual worlds, then on the possible-worlds analysis, these sentences are made true by the fact that there are dogs in the actual world (and in the case of the former sentence, by the fact that there are no other worlds).

[23] This view is similar to Rosen's (1990) modal fictionalism, but it's also importantly different.

Prima facie, it seems that mathematical anti-realists can't endorse this view. For mathematical anti-realists are committed to the idea that certain kinds of modal claims are *true*. And if they endorse modal error theory, they'll have to give this up.

But perhaps mathematical anti-realists can respond to this by maintaining that (a) our modal claims aren't *strictly speaking* true, but (b) they're still *correct* – or *for-all-practical-purposes true* – in some yet-to-be-defined way. I think this is a promising idea. But how is the relevant sort of for-all-practical-purposes truth – let's call it *modal-FAPP-truth* – to be defined?

Before trying to answer this question, let me make two points. First, it seems that *all* modal error theorists – regardless of whether they endorse mathematical anti-realism – *need* a notion of modal-FAPP-truth. For they presumably don't want to just say that our modal sentences are false and leave it at that. Like mathematical error theorists, modal error theorists presumably want to claim that some of our modal sentences are "good" and some are "bad"; for example, they presumably want to claim that sentences like [Possible] (i.e., like 'There could have been flying saucers') are "good" (or modal-FAPP-true), whereas sentences like 'There could have been round squares' are "bad" (or modal-FAPP-false).

Second, modal error theorists presumably also want to claim that modal-FAPP-truth is *objective and factual*. Moreover, it seems in particular that mathematical anti-realists who endorse modal error theory need modal-FAPP-truth to be objective and factual. For we found in the first part of this Element that in order to account for various facts about mathematical practice – most notably, the fact that mathematics is an objective and factual discipline – mathematical anti-realists need to commit to the truth of certain kinds of modal claims. Now, it might be acceptable for anti-realists to maintain that the modal claims in question are merely modal-FAPP-true (in some yet-to-be-defined sense), rather than strictly and literally true, *but only if the relevant sort of modal-FAPP-truth is objective and factual*. Otherwise, they won't be able to account for the objectivity and factualness of mathematics.

Given all this, let me return to the question of how modal-FAPP-truth is to be defined. One way to proceed here would be to define it as follows:

> *Not-Quite-Right Definition*: A sentence is *modal-FAPP-true* iff it would have been true if there had really existed a plenitudinous space of non-actual possible worlds.

But there's an obvious objection to this definition that can be put in the following way:

> *The circularity objection*: To say that a modal sentence is modal-FAPP-true, according to Not-Quite-Right Definition, is to say that a certain *counterfactual* is strictly and literally true. But counterfactuals are *themselves* modal

claims. So how can modal error theorists claim that these counterfactuals are true? After all, modal error theorists are committed to saying that our modal sentences *aren't* true. So they have to say that the counterfactuals at issue here aren't true. And so if modal error theorists use Not-Quite-Right Definition, then they can't say that ordinary modal sentences like [Possible] are modal-FAPP-true.

I think there's a way for modal error theorists to solve this problem. The first step is to endorse the following view:

> *Weak Modal Primitivism:* Even if primitive modal operators don't play a role in ordinary modal discourse, we can *introduce* a primitive modal operator – 'possibly*' – and we can use it to say things like 'Possibly*, there are flying saucers.' This isn't a sentence of English, but we can just stipulate that it's a sentence of *English**, where English* is just like English except that it includes 'possibly*,' 'necessarily*,' and a new counterfactual operator – 'if it had been the case that ..., then it would* have been the case that ... ' – that's either (a) another primitive term or (b) defined in terms of 'possibly*' and 'necessarily*.'

I think weak modal primitivism is pretty obviously true. To reject it, you'd have to say that we *can't* introduce 'possibly*' (or 'would*'), and in order to say that, it seems that you'd have to say that 'possibly*' (or 'would*') is *meaningless*. And that seems really implausible.[24]

Given this, modal error theorists can respond to the circularity objection by defining modal-FAPP-truth as follows:

> *Final Definition*: A sentence is *modal-FAPP-true* iff it would* have been true if there had really existed a plenitudinous space of non-actual possible worlds.

If modal error theorists want to get by without using a counterfactual operator – if they want to just use 'possibly*' and 'necessarily*' – then they could instead use the following definition:

> *Alternative Definition*: A sentence S is *modal-FAPP-true* iff necessarily*, if there really exists a plenitudinous space of non-actual possible worlds, then S is true.

I think there are good reasons for modal error theorists to use Final Definition instead of Alternative Definition – that is, for defining modal-FAPP-truth in terms of the literal truth of counterfactuals, rather than necessitarian conditionals. The reasons are exactly analogous to the reasons I gave in Section 3.6 for

---

[24] You might worry here that even if we can introduce the term 'possibly*,' it doesn't follow that anything *satisfies* this concept – that is, that there are any true sentences of the form 'Possibly*, P.' I agree; but I'll argue in Section 8 that there *are* true sentences of this form.

favoring a counterfactualist definition of FAPP-truth over a necessitarian definition. The main point, in a nutshell, is that the counterfactual definition enables us (and the necessitarian definition doesn't enable us) to endorse a unified view of pure modal sentences like [Possible] and mixed sentences like 'Grass is green, and there could have been flying saucers.' But I won't bother to run through the details of this argument here; I'll just assume that modal error theorists should use Final Definition to define modal-FAPP-truth.

Given all this, modal error theorists can say that the modal-FAPP-truth of ordinary modal sentences is grounded in the literal truth of counterfactuals of English* – that is, counterfactuals that employ the ' ... would* ... ' operator. For instance, to say that [Possible] is modal-FAPP-true, on this view, is to say that the following counterfactual is strictly and literally true:

> [Possible-CF] If there had really existed a plenitudinous space of non-actual possible worlds, then it would* have been the case that there was a possible world containing flying saucers.

But now notice that if modal error theorists endorse this stance, then they have to answer the truthmaking question for sentences like [Possible-CF]. In other words, they have to tell us what *makes* sentences like [Possible-CF] true; they have to tell us what it is about *reality* that makes these sentences true. And this means that while modal error theorists endorse the possible-worlds analysis of ordinary modal discourse, they encounter a truthmaking problem that's more or less equivalent to the truthmaking problem that modal primitivists (i.e., advocates of the primitivist analysis of ordinary modal discourse) encounter.

A similar point can be made about mathematical anti-realists who endorse modal error theory. They need to answer the truthmaking question for counterfactuals like the following:

> [D] If there had really existed a plenitudinous space of non-actual possible worlds, then it would* have been the case that the following counterfactual was true: 'If there had been a plenitudinous realm of abstract objects, then it would have been the case that 3 was prime.'

But this can be simplified. To say that mathematical anti-realists need to answer the truthmaking question for [D] is more or less equivalent to saying that they need to answer the truthmaking question for

> [CF*] If there had actually existed a plenitudinous realm of abstract objects, then it would* have been the case that 3 was prime.

But this is essentially equivalent to what mathematical anti-realists who endorse modal primitivism need to do. They need to answer the truthmaking question for

[CF] If there had actually existed a plenitudinous realm of abstract objects, then it would have been the case that 3 was prime.

The only difference between [CF] and [CF*] is that [CF] contains the English word 'would' instead of the English* word 'would*.' But modal primitivists think those two words are synonymous – and, hence, that [CF] and [CF*] are synonymous. And so it turns out that mathematical anti-realists have to answer the very same truthmaking question, regardless of whether they endorse modal error theory or modal primitivism. In particular, they have to answer the truthmaking question for sentences like [CF*].

6.4 Deflationary Truth and Modality

Mathematical anti-realists might try to endorse an Azzouni-(2010)-style deflationary-truth view of modal discourse according to which (a) ordinary modal sentences like [Possible] are claims about possible worlds, and (b) there are no such things as (non-actual) possible worlds, but despite this, (c) modal sentences like [Possible] are still true.

But there are two problems with this suggestion. First, all the problems with the deflationary-truth nominalist view of mathematics (see Section 2.4.2 for a discussion of these problems) carry over to the deflationary-truth view of modality. In particular, I think it can be argued that the deflationary-truth view of modality (a) involves an empirically implausible view of the ordinary-language meaning of the word 'true' and (b) is not importantly different from modal error theory.

Second, if mathematical anti-realists endorse a deflationary-truth view of modality, they won't be able to account for the factualness, or the objective correctness, of our modal sentences – and so they won't be able to account for the factualness or objective correctness of our mathematical theories. Let me say a few words about this. Deflationary-truth nominalists think that, for example,

[S1] Santa Claus lives at the North Pole

is true despite the fact that there's no such thing as Santa Claus. But now consider

[S2] Santa Claus lives in Cleveland.

Deflationary-truth nominalists don't think [S2] is true. But *why*? Given that there's no such thing as Santa Claus, what's the difference between [S1] and [S2]? The only plausible answer to this question is that the difference has to do with *our conventions*. But now consider these two sentences:

[H1] 17 is the successor of 16.

[H2] 16 doesn't have a successor; rather, 16 is the largest number.

Deflationary-truth nominalists claim that [H1] is true and [H2] is false. But, again, *why*? Given that they think there are no such things as numbers – and, in particular, no such things as 16 or 17 – why do they think [H1] is true and [H2] isn't?

One thing deflationary-truth nominalists could say here is that the difference between [H1] and [H2] has to do with our conventions – *and that's all there is to say on the matter*. But if they endorse that view, then it seems that they won't be able to account for the factualness, or the objective correctness, of our mathematical theories.

As we saw in the first part of this Element, this is precisely why mathematical anti-realists need to commit to modal claims – because they need to account for the difference between sentences like [H1] and sentences like [H2]. Or to use the example I used in the first part of this Element, they need to account for the difference between sentences like '3 is prime' and sentences like '4 is prime.' And they also need to account for the importance of proof in mathematical practice; for example, they need to account for the fact that [H1] and '3 is prime' *follow from* the axioms of arithmetic. Or to put the point differently, they need to account for the fact that if the standard axioms are true, then [H1] and '3 is prime' *must* be true.

But this means that deflationary-truth nominalists can't endorse a conventionalist view of the difference between modal sentences like the following:

[N1] Necessarily, if the axioms of arithmetic are true, then 3 is prime.

[N2] Necessarily, if the axioms of arithmetic are true, then 4 is prime.

Deflationary-truth nominalists claim that [N1] is true, and [N2] is false. But if they endorse a deflationary-truth view of these sentences, then they'll have to say that the difference between [N1] and [N2] is just a *conventional* difference. But if they do that, then they can't say that there's an objective, factual difference between [N1] and [N2]. But then they won't be able to account for the objectivity and factualness of *mathematics*.

Again, this was one of the main points of the first part of this Element. Since anti-realists don't believe in abstract objects, it seems that in order to account for the objectivity and factualness of mathematics, they need to endorse an objective, factualist view of certain kinds of modal claims. This is where the buck needs to stop for mathematical anti-realists, if they're going to account for the fact that mathematics is an objective, factual discipline. And so it seems to me that mathematical anti-realists cannot plausibly endorse the deflationary-truth view of modal discourse articulated in the first paragraph of this section.

6.5 Summing Up

In sum, then, it seems that there's only one tenable way for mathematical anti-realists to endorse the possible-worlds analysis of ordinary modal discourse. They can do this only if they endorse the modal error theory described in Section 6.3. But as we saw in that section, if mathematical anti-realists endorse modal error theory, then they also have to introduce some primitive modal operators – like 'possible*' and 'if it had been the case that ..., then it would* have been the case that ... ' – and they have to commit to the truth of modal sentences involving these primitives, for example, counterfactuals like

> [CF*] If there had actually existed a plenitudinous realm of abstract objects, then it would* have been the case that 3 was prime.

Finally, if mathematical anti-realists endorse a modal error theory of this kind, then they have to answer the truthmaking question for sentences like [CF*]. In other words, they have to tell us what it is about reality that makes these sentences true.

But this is essentially equivalent to what advocates of the primitivist analysis of ordinary modal discourse need to do. And so what we've found in this section is that while mathematical anti-realists *can* endorse the possible-worlds analysis of ordinary modal discourse – by also endorsing modal error theory – if they do this, they'll encounter the very same truthmaking question that's encountered by anti-realists who endorse the primitivist analysis of ordinary modal discourse. And so I'll turn now to the question of whether mathematical anti-realists can *answer* this truthmaking question about sentences that involve primitive modal operators.

7 Modal Primitivism

7.1 Opening Remarks

Modal primitivism is the view that the primitivist analysis of ordinary modal discourse is true – that is, that ordinary modal claims are best interpreted as involving primitive modal operators. One way to develop this view is to introduce the terms 'possibly*' and 'necessarily*' and to stipulate that the former is a primitive sentential possibility operator and the latter is a sentential necessity operator that's defined in terms of the former. Given this, modal primitivists can say that, for example,

> [Possible] There could have been flying saucers

is equivalent to

[Possible*] Possibly*, there are flying saucers.[25]

Moreover, as we've seen, mathematical anti-realists who endorse modal primitivism will probably also want to maintain that counterfactuals involve a primitive counterfactual operator, namely, 'if it had been the case that ...., then it would* have been the case that .... .' (Or at any rate, anti-realists who endorse counterfactual FAPP-ist error theory, or counterfactual if-thenism, will want to do this.)[26]

In this section, I'll discuss two questions. First, how should modal primitivists answer the truthmaking question for ordinary modal sentences like [Possible]? In other words, the first question is just this:

> Assuming that modal primitivism is true, what makes sentences like [Possible] true? In particular, what is it about *reality* that makes these sentences true?

One point to note here is that it's not at all obvious what the answer to this question could be. We saw in Section 6 that the possible-worlds analysis of ordinary modal discourse brings with it an answer to the truthmaking question. But the primitivist analysis doesn't do this. Indeed, by itself, modal primitivism doesn't tell us *anything* about how to answer the truthmaking question. It tells us that [Possible] is equivalent to [Possible*], but it doesn't tell us what makes [Possible] true because it doesn't tell us what makes [Possible*] true. And it's not as if it's obvious what makes [Possible*] true; indeed, it's totally unclear.

The second question I'll discuss in this section is the following: Is there any modal primitivist answer to the truthmaking question that's available to mathematical anti-realists? Mathematical anti-realists are committed to the truth of very specific kinds of modal sentences; in particular, the best versions of the view are committed to the truth of sentences of one of the following two kinds:

> [CF] If there had actually existed a plenitudinous realm of abstract objects, then it would have been the case that 3 was prime.

> [N] Necessarily, if there exists a plenitudinous realm of abstract objects, then 3 is prime.

So the second question I want to ask in the present section is just this:

---

[25] Views of this kind have been endorsed by Forbes (1989), Shalkowski (1994), and Bueno and Shalkowski (2009).

[26] Actually, as we saw in Section 5.2.2, anti-realists can try to claim that ' ... would* ... ' can be defined in terms of 'possibly*' and 'necessarily*'; but I think anti-realists are better off taking ' ... would* ... ' to be a primitive.

If mathematical anti-realists endorse modal primitivism, is there any tenable way for them to answer the truthmaking question for sentences like [CF] and [N]?

I am going to argue in Sections 7.3–7.7 that mathematical anti-realists don't seem to have any viable options here. But before I do this, I need to clarify something about the notion of possibility*.

7.2 Possibility* as the Broadest Kind of Possibility

According to the modal primitivist view that I've got in mind, 'possible*' expresses the broadest kind of possibility. But more needs to be said than this because there are multiple ways of thinking about what the broadest kind of possibility *is*. One view here – which I won't end up endorsing – is the following:

The broadest kind of possibility is *logical* possibility (where, roughly speaking, a sentence S is *logically possible* iff there's at least one interpretation of S's nonlogical vocabulary on which S is true). Now, of course, we can define other (narrower) notions of possibility; for example, the *conceptual* possibilities form a subset of the logical possibilities, and the *metaphysical* possibilities form a subset of the conceptual possibilities. So, for example, 'Water isn't made of H_2O' is logically and conceptually possible but not metaphysically possible; and 'Some bachelors are married' is logically possible but not conceptually or metaphysically possible. But there's nothing that's possible in one of these other ways but not logically possible.

It seems to me, however, that so-called "logical possibility" isn't a genuine kind of *possibility* at all. After all, the sentence 'There are some married bachelors' is logically possible, but the existence of married bachelors is, in fact, *not possible*. (The reason that 'There are some married bachelors' is logically possible is that it would be true if we interpreted it to say that, for instance, there are some yellow cars; but the proposition that's actually expressed by this sentence is straightforwardly impossible.)

Likewise, I think that so-called "conceptual possibility" isn't a genuine kind of possibility either. For (a) 'There is some non-H_2O Water' is conceptually possible, but (b) the existence of non-H_2O water isn't possible.

What, then, do I mean when I talk about "the broadest kind of possibility"? The easiest way to understand the sort of possibility that I've got in mind here is to assume for a moment that Lewisian possible worlds really exist (i.e., that the full plenitude of Lewisian worlds exists) and to think of the broadest kind of possibility as the kind of possibility picked out by the concept *true in at least one Lewisian world*. This view correctly implies that married bachelors and non-H_2O water are not possible – because there aren't any Lewisian worlds that contain married bachelors or non-H_2O water (although, of course, there *are* Lewisian worlds where we use 'water' to denote CO_2 and where we use 'married' and 'bachelor' to express the concepts *yellow* and *car*, respectively).

It's important to note, however, that I'm not committing here to the real existence of Lewisian worlds. What we can say is that the kind of possibility that I've got in mind (namely, *possibility**) is coextensive with the concept *true in at least one Lewisian world* – or, more precisely, that it *would* (or *would**) have been coextensive with that concept if realism about Lewisian words had been true. Or more simply: the kind of possibility that I've got in mind is the kind that applies to a sentence S just in case S would (or would*) have been true in at least one Lewisian world if the whole plenitudinous space of Lewisian worlds had really existed.

I'll say more in Sections 8.2.3–8.2.4 about the kind of possibility that 'possible*' expresses; but for now, this is good enough.

7.3 Why Analyticity Doesn't Help

It might seem that modal primitivists can make progress on the truthmaking question for [Possible] and [Possible*] by arguing that these sentences are *analytic* (or true in virtue of meaning, or some such thing). In order to endorse this line, you'd have to commit to both of the following claims:

> *Modal Analyticism:* Some modal sentences – for example, [Possible] and [Possible*] – are analytic, or true in virtue of meaning, or some such thing.[27]

> *Analyticity-to-the-Rescue:* The claim that sentences like [Possible] and [Possible*] are analytic helps with the truthmaking question for these sentences (i.e., the question of what it is about reality that makes these sentences true).

I think modal analyticism might be true – the view seems prima facie plausible to me – but analyticity-to-the-rescue is false. To see why, consider the following sentence that's presumably analytic:

> [Round or Not Round] Mars is round or it's not the case that Mars is round.

This sentence is analytic, if any sentence is. And so it might seem that it's made true by facts about meaning, or our conventions. But it's not. Facts about our conventions only make it the case that [Round or Not Round] means in English that Mars is round or it's not the case that Mars is round; they don't also make it

---

[27] See, for example, Forbes (1985), Sidelle (1989), Ludwig (n.d.), and Thomasson (2020) for views in the neighborhood of modal analyticism.

the case that this is *true*. We can bring this out by reflecting on ordinary nonanalytic sentences like

[Red] Mars is red.

There's a sense in which [Red] is made true partially by our conventions (in particular, by the conventions that make it the case that [Red] means in English that Mars is red) and partially by the worldly fact that Mars is red. But we don't bother to say this. We just say that it's made true by the fact that Mars is red. This is because when we talk about truthmaking, we're not talking about the conventional facts that make the sentences in question mean what they do; we're talking about the worldly facts that make these sentences true, *given what they mean*. So when we say that [Red] is made true by the fact that Mars is red, what we mean is this: *given what this sentence means*, it's made true by the fact that Mars is red. Thus, when we ask what makes [Round or Not Round] true, we're asking this: *Given what this sentence means*, what makes it true? And once we recognize this, it makes no sense to say that this sentence is made true by our conventions.[28]

But there's an obvious line we can take on what makes [Round or Not Round] true. This sentence is a disjunction, and one of its disjuncts – namely, 'Mars is round' – is true. So [Round or Not Round] is made true by the fact that Mars is round (or, if you don't like reified facts, it's made true by Mars and how Mars is, namely, by its being round). Now, of course, if Mars weren't round, then [Round or Not Round] would still be true, and in that scenario, it would be made true by something else; but it's *actually right now* made true by the fact that Mars is round.

(You might wonder: if analytic sentences like [Round or Not Round] aren't made true by facts about meaning, then how can we say that they're true *in virtue of* meaning? The answer, I think, is that we can say that these sentences are true "in virtue of" meaning because they *follow from* true claims about meaning – or if you prefer, because they can be *explained by* true claims about meaning.)

The important point, though, is that the fact that [Round or Not Round] is analytic is totally irrelevant to the truthmaking question. We answer the truthmaking question for [Round or Not Round] in the same way that we answer it for true disjunctions that *aren't* analytic – for example, 'Mars is round or snow is green.'

---

[28] Arguments in this ballpark have been advanced by Lewy (1976), Boghossian (1997), Sider (2003), and Williamson (2007). For a response, see Thomasson (2009). Also, Warren (2015) defends a kind of conventionalism against arguments of this kind, but he wouldn't say that analytic sentences are *made true* by our conventions. Finally, Quine (1983) also argues against truth by convention.

Given this result, it seems that modal primitivists can't use an appeal to analyticity to answer the truthmaking question for modal sentences like [Possible] and [Possible*]. For even if we assume that these sentences *are* analytic, it's totally unclear what makes them true, if the primitivist analysis of ordinary modal discourse is correct. Moreover, we can't answer the truth-making question for these sentences in anything like the way that we answer it for nonmodal analytic sentences like [Round or Not Round]. For (a) we answer the truthmaking question for nonmodal analytic sentences like [Round or Not Round] by appealing to ordinary contingent facts about the actual world (e.g., the fact that Mars is round), and (b) there don't seem to be any facts of this kind that could make sentences like [Possible] and [Possible*] true.

So modal primitivists have to look elsewhere for an answer to the truthmaking question for sentences like [Possible] and [Possible*].

7.4 Sider-Style Conventionalism

We just saw in Section 7.3 that we can't plausibly maintain that modal sentences are made true by our conventions. But there's another sort of conventionalism that's worth considering here, namely, Sider's (2003, 2011) view (and see also Cameron (2009a)). On Sider's view, roughly speaking, 'Necessarily p' is true if and only if (i) 'p' is true, and (ii) it's a logical truth, or an analytic truth, or a mathematical sentence, or what might be called a Kripkean sentence (e.g., 'Water is H$_2$O,' 'Ali is Clay,' 'Ali is human,' etc.), or a metaphysical principle (e.g., mereological universalism), or . . . etc., etc., etc. Thus, on Sider's view, sentences of the form 'Necessarily p' aren't *true* by convention, but they *are* necessary by convention; in other words, which kinds of truths count as necessary is a matter of convention. So in connection with the truthmaking question, the idea would be that 'Necessarily p' is made true by (a) whatever makes 'p' true, and (b) our conventions surrounding 'necessarily' – or something like that.

The problem with this view, from the point of view of mathematical anti-realism, is analogous to the problem that I brought out for deflationary-truth views in Section 6.4. If mathematical anti-realists endorse a Sider-style conventionalist view of modality, then they won't be able to account for the factualness and objectivity of mathematics. We can appreciate this by considering the following four sentences:

[P1] If there exists a plenitudinous realm of abstract objects, then 3 is prime.

[P2] If there exists a plenitudinous realm of abstract objects, then 4 is prime.

[P3] Necessarily, if there exists a plenitudinous realm of abstract objects, then 3 is prime.

[P4] Necessarily, if there exists a plenitudinous realm of abstract objects, then 4 is prime.

Since mathematical anti-realists don't believe in mathematical objects, they have to say that [P1] and [P2] are both true. That's fine. But in order to account for the factualness and objectivity of mathematics, anti-realists need to be able to claim that [P3] and [P4] have different truth values; in particular, they need to maintain that [P3] is true and [P4] is false; and they need the difference between these two sentences to be factual and objective. But given that anti-realists think that [P1] and [P2] are both true, it follows that if they endorse Sider's view of modality, then they'll have to say that the difference in truth value between [P3] and [P4] is a matter of *convention*; and so they won't be able to account for the fact that there's an objective and factual difference between [P3] and [P4] – or between '3 is prime' and '4 is prime.'

More generally, I think similar remarks can be made about *all* conventionalist views of modality. In short, it seems that if mathematical anti-realists endorse a conventionalist view of modality, then they won't be able to account for the factualness and objectivity of mathematics.

7.5 Essentialism

One idea that modal primitivists might pursue is that modal claims are made true by the *essences* of objects. Consider, for example, the following sentence:

[O1] Necessarily, if Obama exists, then he's human.

You might think that Obama is *essentially* human – or that he has the property *being human* essentially – and, hence, that he couldn't exist without having that property. And you might think that this is what makes [O1] true.[29]

One problem with essentialist views of this kind – not the most important problem in the context of this Element – is that they're metaphysically extravagant, and they're incompatible with a physicalistic, materialistic worldview. I think that a lot of philosophers would say that it's just obvious that views of this kind – that is, views that imply that there are objects that have properties like *being human* essentially – are metaphysically extravagant and immaterialistic. But here's a quick argument for this claim:

> It seems clear that the pile of physical matter that constitutes Obama is *not* essentially human – because that matter could be reorganized so that it no longer had the property *being human*. Therefore, essentialist views of the kind at issue here – in particular, views that imply that Obama is essentially

---

[29] Views of this general kind are endorsed by Fine (2005) and Lowe (n.d.).

human – seem to imply that Obama is numerically distinct from the matter that constitutes him. And so these views seem to imply that Obama is not a purely physical, material thing – that there's something more to him than the physical matter that constitutes him. Moreover, this result generalizes. In order for essentialist views of the above kind to work – in order for them to provide us with a general account of what makes our modal claims true – they'll have to say that there are objects that have properties like *being a table* and *being a car* essentially. So views of this kind imply that ordinary objects like my table and my car are numerically distinct from the matter that constitutes them, and so they imply that my table and my car are not purely physical, material things. Therefore, essentialist views of the kind at issue here are incompatible with physicalism and materialism.

Now, you might respond to this by just endorsing a metaphysically extravagant and immaterialistic view. But, remember, we're hunting for a view of modality that mathematical anti-realists can endorse. And perhaps the primary appeal of mathematical anti-realism is that it gives us a way to deny the existence of abstract objects. Presumably the people who endorse this view are motivated by the desire to avoid metaphysical extravagance. So I don't think many mathematical anti-realists would endorse an essentialist view of the kind at issue here.

Nevertheless, it seems to me that essentialism is strictly *compatible* with mathematical anti-realism, and so anti-realists *could* endorse this view if they wanted to.

But there's a much worse problem lurking nearby. As we've seen, mathematical anti-realists are committed to modal claims of a very specific kind. In particular, they're committed to the truth of sentences like the following:

[CF] If there had actually existed a plenitudinous realm of abstract objects, then it would have been the case that 3 was prime.

[N] Necessarily, if there exists a plenitudinous realm of abstract objects, then 3 is prime.

But how on Earth could sentences like [CF] and [N] be made true by essential properties of the objects that mathematical anti-realists believe in? If anti-realists believed in *numbers*, then they could of course say that [CF] and [N] are made true by essential properties of those objects. But anti-realists *don't* believe in numbers. Or any other abstract objects. They believe in physical objects like Mars and mental objects like the pain in my toe. But none of these objects seems to have any essential properties that could make sentences like [CF] and [N] true.

Perhaps you think that the *universe* has the property *being such that [CF] and [N] are true* essentially – and that this is what makes [CF] and [N] true. This has the ring of a desperate maneuver – something someone would say when they've been backed into a corner – and I think that's exactly what it is. One point to note here is that the essentialist view of modal truthmaking – that is, of what makes modal sentences true – can succeed only if 'essential property' isn't defined in modal terms; for instance, essentialists can't say (with, for example, Kripke (1980)) that an object O has the property P *essentially* if and only if (and by definition) O couldn't exist without having P. Instead, essentialists have to say (with, for example, Fine (1994)) that O has P *essentially* iff (and by definition) P is part of the very *nature* of O, or what it *is* to be O, or some such thing. So, for example, on this view, while it's true that Obama couldn't exist without having the property *being such that all cats are cats*, this isn't an essential property of Obama because it's not part of what it *is* to be Obama. But given this, it's hard to see how mathematical anti-realists could plausibly endorse the view mentioned in the first sentence of this paragraph. For if we let 'U' denote the physical universe, it's hard to see how mathematical anti-realists – philosophers who, remember, don't believe in abstract objects – could claim with a straight face that the property *being such that [CF] and [N] are true* is part of the very *nature* of U, or part of what it *is* to be U. This is a desperate and bizarre view that I don't think any mathematical anti-realist would want to endorse.

I think that considerations like this generalize and create problems for *all* modal primitivists who try to answer the truthmaking problem for their view by endorsing an essentialist view of the above kind – regardless of whether they also endorse mathematical anti-realism. For its hard to see how essentialist modal primitivists could account for the truth of sentences like

[DM] There could have been totally different matter than there actually is.

But I won't try to argue for this here. I'll just stick with the point I've already made – that there doesn't seem to be any tenable way for mathematical anti-realists to claim that sentences like [CF] and [N] are made true by facts about the essential properties of the concrete objects that they believe in.

7.6 Powers and Potentialities

Similar remarks can be made about the view that ordinary modal sentences are made true by powers, or potentialities. Consider, for example, the following sentence:

[O2] Obama could go for a walk.

You might think that Obama has the *power* to go for a walk – or that he has the *potentiality* to go for a walk – and you might think that this is what makes [O2] true.[30]

Perhaps. But it's hard to see how we could account for the truth of [DM] by appealing to powers or potentialities. Does anything have (or did anything ever have) the power or potentiality to be such that totally different matter existed? It seems not. And so it's hard to see how advocates of powers and/or potentiality views can account for the truth of [DM].

But what really matters in the present context is that *mathematical anti-realists* can't use a powers or potentiality view to account for the truth of sentences like [CF] and [N]. If we assume with mathematical anti-realists that there are no abstract objects – and, in particular, no numbers – then does anything in the universe have the power or potentiality to be such that [CF] and [N] are true? Perhaps you think that *everything* has a power or potentiality of that sort. Perhaps you think that, for example, *Obama* does. But even if that's true, that is surely a trivial, nonsubstantive feature of Obama. It may be that Obama has the property *being such that snow is white*; but this is surely not what makes 'Snow is white' true. That sentence is *independently* true. And likewise, even if Obama has the power or potentiality to be such that [CF] is true, that is not what makes [CF] true. [CF] has to be true independently of Obama. And it seems that similar remarks can be made about all of the objects that mathematical anti-realists believe in – for those objects are all just specific concrete objects like Obama.

7.7 Generalizing

The arguments of Sections 7.5 and 7.6 seem to me to generalize. If we assume with mathematical anti-realists that there are no abstract objects (and, in particular, no numbers) – that is, if we assume that all objects are ordinary concrete objects like Obama and Mars and the pain in my toe – then it's hard to see how sentences like [CF] and [N] could be made true by facts about existent objects. Mars doesn't seem to have *any* properties that make [CF] or [N] true. And neither does Obama, and neither does the pain in my toe. There don't seem to be any facts about any objects in the physical world – any objects that mathematical anti-realists believe in – that could make sentences like [CF] and [N] true.

So mathematical anti-realists seem to be in trouble. We found in the first part of this Element that anti-realists need to claim that sentences like [CF] and [N] are true. But the arguments of this section and the preceding section suggest that anti-realists don't have any story to tell about what makes these sentences true.

However, I think there's a way out of this pickle. In the next section, I'll explain how anti-realists can answer the truthmaking question for modal claims.

---

[30] This view is defended by Vetter (2018).

8 Modal Nothingism to the Rescue

8.1 Opening Remarks

We found in the first part of this Element that mathematical anti-realists are committed to the truth of modal sentences like the following:

[CF] If there had actually existed a plenitudinous realm of abstract objects, then it would have been the case that 3 was prime.

[N] Necessarily, if there exists a plenitudinous realm of abstract objects, then 3 is prime.

But the discussion in Sections 6–7 seems to suggest that anti-realists don't have access to any plausible view of what makes these sentences true (i.e., of what it is about *reality* that makes them true).

Given this, you might think we should just give up on mathematical anti-realism. But in this section, I'll explain how anti-realists can solve this problem. In other words, I'll explain how they can answer the truthmaking question for modal sentences like [CF] and [N]. I'll do this by arguing for a view that I'll call *modal nothingism*.

I'll start off by focusing on simple modal sentences like

[Possible] There could have been flying saucers.

This will make it easier to articulate and argue for modal nothingism. But in Section 8.6, I'll argue that we can endorse a modal nothingist view of sentences like [CF] and [N] as well – and that this gives mathematical anti-realists a solution to the modal truthmaking problem with their view.

It's important to note that modal nothingism is *semantically neutral*. In particular, as will become clear in Sections 8.6–8.7, modal nothingism can be combined with (a) modal primitivism – that is, the primitivist analysis of ordinary modal discourse – or (b) the possible-worlds analysis of that discourse, or (c) the view that in Section 5.2.3 I called Hybrid-Mess-ism.

8.2 What Is Modal Nothingism?

8.2.1 Initial Statement of the Theory

Let 'possibly*' be a primitive sentential possibility operator – in particular, let it express the *broadest* kind of possibility (see Section 7.2 for more on this) – and consider the following sentence:

[Possible*] Possibly*, there are flying saucers.

According to modal primitivism, [Possible] is equivalent to [Possible*]. But for the time being, we needn't worry about this. Because modal nothingism doesn't say anything about any ordinary-language sentences like [Possible] or [CF] or [N]. It makes claims only about sentences like [Possible*]. Or to put the point differently, modal nothingism doesn't say anything about *English*; it makes claims only about *English**, where English* is just like English except that it includes 'possibly*' and 'necessarily*' and a primitive counterfactual operator 'if it had been the case that . . . , then it would* have been the case that . . . .'[31] In particular, we can formulate modal nothingism as follows:

> *Modal Nothingism*: (I) Sentences like [Possible*] are substantively true. And (II) there's *nothing* about reality that makes them true. Or perhaps better: reality doesn't have any substantive features that make it the case that sentences like [Possible*] are true. There's no stuff that makes them true; there are no objects that make them true; and there are no features of any existent things that make them true.[32]

It's important to note that thesis (II) is stronger than the mere claim that [Possible*] doesn't have a truthmaker. Thesis (II) tells us that there's no truthmak*ing* in connection with sentences like [Possible*]. In other words, it tells us that the following principle is false:

> *All Truths are Made True by Reality (or for short, TMR):* For any true sentence S, there's something about reality (or about how things are in reality, or some such thing) that *makes S true*. Put differently, the idea here is that S is made true by (a) what exists and (b) how the existent things are.

Modal nothingism implies that TMR is false. This might seem implausible. Indeed, TMR might seem so obviously true that you might wonder how it could be false. And you might wonder whether denying TMR commits us to a deflationary-truth view of modal discourse. But in Section 8.3, I'll explain how TMR could be false; and in Sections 8.4–8.5, I'll argue that it in fact *is*

---

[31] If you like, you can try to define ' . . . would* . . . ' in terms of 'possibly*' and 'necessarily*'; but for present purposes, we can assume that ' . . . would* . . . ' is a primitive. For more on this, see Section 5.2.2.

[32] I first introduced this view in "Fictionalism, Mathematical Facts, and Logical Facts" (Balaguer 2010), and developed it more fully in *Metaphysics, Sophistry, and Illusion* (Balaguer 2021). As far as I know, the view was original there. But Tallant (2009) defends a view that's somewhat similar. Moreover, I suspect that modal analyticists like Forbes (1985), Sidelle (1989), and Ludwig (n.d.) – see Section 7.3 for an articulation of modal analyticism – would probably be happy to endorse something like modal nothingism. But to the best of my knowledge, none of them has ever articulated the view, much less argued for it. Finally, it's worth noting that, because of thesis (I), modal nothingism is very different from the conventionalist views of people like Sider (2003, 2011), Thomasson (2020), and Azzouni (2010).

false; and in Section 8.9, I'll explain why this doesn't commit us to a deflationary-truth view of modality.

Before I do any of this, however, I want to say more to develop the modal nothingist view. And I want to start by saying a few words to clarify thesis (I) of modal nothingism. When I say that [Possible*] is *substantively* true, I mean at least three things. First, it isn't vacuously true, or true in an empty way, along the lines of, say, 'All unicorns are purple.' Second, [Possible*] *says* something; in other words, it goes out on a limb and makes a truth-evaluable *claim.* Now, as we'll see in Sections 8.3–8.5, I don't think [Possible*] makes a claim about *reality*, or about how things *are*; rather, on the view I'll be developing, it makes a claim about how things *could have been*. Third and most important, on the view I've got in mind, [Possible*] is *objectively* true. And it's true *independently of us and our conventions*; even if we had never existed, it would still be the case that, possibly*, there are flying saucers.

8.2.2 The Scope of Modal Nothingism

As it's formulated above, modal nothingism is about sentences that are "like [Possible*]". I want to make this a bit more precise. The first point to note here is that I don't endorse a nothingist view of *all* sentences involving 'possibly*' and 'necessarily*' and 'would*.' Consider, for example, the following sentences:

[W] Necessarily*, if there's a sample of water, then there's a sample of H_2O.

[O] Obama is such that, possibly*, he's a republican.

[C] If my glass had been filled with water, then it would* have been filled with H_2O.

I don't endorse a nothingist view of these sentences. I think [W] and [C] are made true partially by the fact that the watery stuff in our environment – the stuff in our lakes and pipes and so on – is made of H_2O.[33] And I think [O] is made true partially by the fact that Obama exists.

(Notice that I'm saying that [W] and [O] and [C] are made true *partially* by worldly facts. This is because I think there's an aspect of the truth of these sentences – a purely modal part of their truth – that's made true by nothing. I think there's a general theory to be developed here of *de re* modal claims and sentences that involve metaphysical but not conceptual necessities – a theory

---

[33] [W] and [C] are also made true partially by the fact that we use the word 'water' as a rigid designator. But this can be thought of as a meaning fact, and as we've seen, truthmaking questions aren't really about the meaning facts that make our sentences true; they're about the non-meaning facts, or the worldly facts, that make our sentences true.

that holds that there are purely modal parts of these sentences that are made true by nothing (or perhaps better, that these sentences are made true partially by nothing). But this isn't the place to develop this theory.[34])

So which modal truths is modal nothingism about? What do I mean by "sentences like [Possible*]"? Well, one way to put the view here – and I'm fine with this way of putting it – is that modal nothingism is about sentences of the form 'Necessarily* P' or 'Possibly* P' or 'If it had been the case that . . . , then it would* have been the case that . . . ' that are *analytic*. But you don't have to put it this way if you don't want to; if you're not a fan of analyticity, you can take modal nothingism to be about sentences of one of the above three forms that should be thought to be analytic by advocates of modal analyticism. This is clearly not all sentences involving 'possibly*' and 'necessarily*' and 'would*.' Even if you endorse modal analyticism, you shouldn't say that sentences like [W], [O], and [C] are analytic. [O] isn't analytic because it has an existential commitment, and [W] and [C] aren't analytic because there's no analytic link between 'water' and 'H$_2$O.' But if you're attracted to modal analyticism, then I think you should say that [Possible*] is analytic, and, even more obviously, you should say that sentences like the following are analytic:

> [Necessary*] Necessarily*, if there are flying, talking donkeys, then there are flying donkeys.

You might be puzzled by the idea that sentences like [Possible*] and [Necessary*] are analytic; I'll say a few words to clarify and motivate this stance in Section 8.2.4.

Now, you might complain that it's not entirely clear *which* sentences of one of these forms – that is, of the form 'Necessarily* P' or 'Possibly* P' or 'If it had been the case that . . . , then it would* have been the case that . . . ' – should be thought to be analytic by advocates of modal analyticism. But (a) this will become more clear as we proceed, and (b) for our purposes here, we don't need very much precision on the exact scope of modal nothingism; all that will matter here is that we can endorse a modal nothingist view of the specific modal sentences that mathematical anti-realists are committed to – and it will become clear as we proceed that we can.

8.2.3 Bruteness and Explanation

Modal nothingists say that there's nothing about reality that makes sentences like [Necessary*] and [Possible*] true. But they don't have to say that these sentences are all *brutely* true; they can say that we can explain the truth of

---

[34] In developing this theory, modal nothingists can make use of some of the insights of Forbes (1985) and Sidelle (1989).

some of these sentences by appealing to more basic modal truths. For instance, one might explain why [Necessary*] is true by saying something like this:

> If [Necessary*] is false, then it's possible* that there both are and aren't flying donkeys; but it's not possible* that there both are and aren't flying donkeys because it's not possible* that there are true contradictions.

Thus, the idea here is that we can explain why [Necessary*] is true by appealing to a more basic modal truth like

> [C1] It's not possible* that there are true contradictions.

And we might try to explain why [Possible*] is true in a similar way. It's not obvious what the best way of doing this is, but one idea is to do it by appealing to a principle that links possibility* to non-contradictoriness. I think that any such principle would need to be pretty complicated – with a bunch of caveats and provisos – to have any hope of being literally true. But perhaps something like the following could do the trick:

> [C2] If there had been a plenitudinous platonic realm of abstract objects like propositions and sentences and contradictions and so on, then it would* have been the case that the following conditional was true: 'If no contradiction follows from a sentence S, even when we combine it with all of the analytic truths – and if there are no rigid designators in S, and if S isn't so imprecise that there's no fact of the matter whether it's true – then it's possible* that S is true.'[35]

For our purposes, it doesn't matter *which* modal truths are the basic modal truths, or the *bottom-level* modal truths, and it doesn't matter whether [C1] and [C2] are such truths. What matters is the more general point that modal nothingists can say that there's a relatively small set of modal truths that are *basic*, or *bottom level*, in the sense that they can be used to explain the truth of all of the other modal truths that modal nothingism is about.

If modal nothingists proceed in this way, then they can say that the only modal truths that are brutely true are the basic modal truths. Now, you might think that there's something wrong with saying that the basic modal truths are brute, but it seems to me that we *all* have to accept the existence of brute truths

---

[35] I'm talking here about sentence *tokens*. And I'm thinking of sentence tokens as having their meanings fixed by the *actual* situation. So, for example, if I utter a token of the sentence 'There are round squares,' and if I'm speaking English, then on the way I'm thinking of things here, it's not possible* that this token is true – even though it *is* possible* that this token means something else and is, for that reason, true.

in this general vicinity, regardless of whether we endorse modal nothingism. Consider, for example, Lewis; he has to say that it's a brute fact that there are no worlds containing true contradictions, and so he's no better off here than modal nothingists who claim that [C1] is brutely true.

8.2.4 Epistemology

Modal nothingism helps make modal epistemology more tractable. In particular, it helps explain how we humans could know that modal sentences like [Possible*] are true because it enables us to say that (i) we don't need to know anything about reality in order to know that sentences like [Possible*] are true; and (ii) sentences like [Possible*] are analytic and, hence, *a priori*; and (iii) sentences like [Possible*] can be deduced from a small set of basic modal truths together with conceptual knowledge; and (iv) because possibility* is the *broadest* kind of possibility, and because nothing is required of reality for sentences like [Possible*] to be true, conceivability is a (defeasible, prima facie) guide to possibility*.

In connection with claim (iv), the idea isn't that conceivability is an *infallible* guide to possibility*; rather, the idea is that if a claim P seems easily conceivable to us, and if we have no reason to doubt that it's possible* – if no one has come along and argued that we're making a mistake vis-à-vis the conceivability/possibility* of P – then that gives us a defeasible prima facie reason to think that P is possible*. Now, you might wonder how we could know that conceivability is a guide to possibility* in even this defeasible way. The answer is that this falls out of the stipulation that 'possible*' expresses the *broadest* kind of possibility – that is, the kind of possibility that's governed by principles like [C1] and [C2] and that people like Lewis are trying to give an account of. There are, of course, other (more restricted) kinds of possibility (e.g., nomological possibility), but 'possible*' just doesn't express them. (There are also broader notions (e.g., so-called "logical possibility"), but as we saw in Section 7.2, this isn't a genuine kind of *possibility* at all.) In any event, given that 'possible*' expresses this extremely broad kind of possibility – a kind of possibility that's coextensive with the concept *true in at least one Lewisian world* (or, more precisely, that *would* (or *would**) be coextensive with that concept if Lewisian worlds really existed) – we can have a pretty good handle on what's possible* and what isn't. For example, it seems pretty *obvious* that flying saucers are possible*. One way to appreciate this is to notice that (a) there's nothing contradictory about the idea of a flying saucer, and (b) glossing over the provisos mentioned in [C2], that's all that's needed for possibility*.

It's worth noting that these remarks point us toward an argument for the claim that modal truths like [Possible*] and [Necessary*] – and, indeed, [C1] and [C2] – are *analytic*. For the claim that these sentences are analytic seems to fall out of the fact that we're talking here about the very broad kind of possibility that's governed by principles like [C1] and [C2], or whatever the basic modal truths turn out to be. In short, the idea here is that (a) the basic modal truths are, in some sense, built into the meanings of 'possibly*' and 'necessarily*'; and (b) this gives us the result that the basic modal truths – and sentences like [Possible*] and [Necessary*] – are analytic.

Finally, these considerations also help modal nothingists explain how we humans could acquire knowledge of the basic modal truths. For if the basic modal truths are analytic, then that surely helps explain how we could know that they're true.

8.3 How Modal Nothingism Could Be True (and How TMR Could Be False)

You might wonder how TMR could be false – that is, how a sentence could be true even if there were nothing about reality that made it true. As a first step toward explaining how TMR could be false, let me start by acknowledging that there's a nearby principle – a slightly restricted version of TMR – that I think is true. To see what I've got in mind here, consider the following two claims:

> *TMR:* For any true sentence S, there's something about reality (or about how things are in reality) that makes S true.

> *TMR-restricted:* For any true sentence S *that's about reality* (or about *how things are* in reality), there's something about reality (or about how things are in reality) that makes S true.

I think that TMR-restricted is not just true, but obviously true. And I think the reason TMR seems so plausible to us, when we first look at it, is that we're over-generalizing from some other principle, like TMR-restricted, that's true.

But the main point I want to make here is that if we look at the way that TMR-restricted is restricted, we're led to an interpretation of sentences like [Possible*] that explains how modal nothingism could be true – and how the unrestricted version of TMR could be false. According to the interpretation I have in mind, sentences like [Possible*] *aren't about reality*; they don't make claims about what *is*, or about how things *are*; rather, they make claims about how things *could have been*.

(Don't read anything into my use of the word 'things' in the expression 'how things could have been.' I'm not committing here to the existence of *some things* and saying that [Possible*] makes a claim about how *those things* could have been. The point can be made without the use of the word 'things'; the point is that, on the reading I have in mind, [Possible*] makes a pure *could-have-been* claim and not a *reality-is-thus-and-so* claim.)

I think that if it's even *possible* to make a claim about how things could have been – or to make a pure could-have-been claim – without making a claim about how things *are*, then we'll have not just an explanation of how modal nothingism could be true, but an argument for the claim that it *is* true.

I want to argue for this by putting [Possible*] on the back burner and focusing on a fictional linguistic community in which [Possible] is equivalent to [Possible*]. In particular, let's imagine that we've discovered a town in Antarctica whose inhabitants (*the Literali*) grew up in total isolation from all other humans but, quite surprisingly, speak a language (*Literese*) that's very similar to English. After we encounter the Literali, our linguists start studying their language, and during their investigation, they ask the Literali about sentences like [Possible] (i.e., sentences like 'There could have been flying saucers'), and they find that the Literali endorse <*modal nothingism*>, where <modal nothingism> is just like modal nothingism except that it's about the Literese sentence [Possible], and sentences like it, instead of sentences like [Possible*]. The linguists are puzzled by this, and they ask the Literali to explain. In response, the Literali produce the following argument for <modal nothingism>, endorsed by every member of their community.

8.4 The Literali's Argument For <Modal Nothingism>

"We'll argue here for a <modal nothingist> view of our sentence [Possible] (i.e., 'There could have been flying saucers') and assume that analogous arguments can be made about other sentences that are similar to [Possible]. And we'll start by explaining what [Possible] says in Literese. The first point to note is that in our language, the primitivist analysis of modal discourse is true, so that [Possible] is equivalent in our language to 'Possibly, there are flying saucers,' where 'possibly' is a primitive sentential possibility operator. But the more important point here is that in our language, [Possible] doesn't say anything about reality, or about how things in reality *are*. It doesn't even imply that reality *exists*. Indeed, it doesn't imply that *anything* exists. It also doesn't ascribe any properties to anything, and it doesn't say that any objects stand in any relations to one another. In short, in our language, [Possible] doesn't say *anything* about *any* existent thing whatsoever.

"You might think that [Possible] says at least *one* thing about reality because you might think it says that *reality is such that there could have been flying saucers*. But in our language, [Possible] *doesn't* say this. Many of us think that reality *is* such that there could have been flying saucers – that is, that reality has that property – but we *all* agree that [Possible] doesn't *say* that reality has that property. You can appreciate this by reflecting on the following: (i) if you think that *reality* is such that there could have been flying saucers, then you presumably also think that *Madonna* is such that there could have been flying saucers; but (ii) [Possible] doesn't *say* that Madonna has that property. So even if it's true that reality has that property, it doesn't follow that [Possible] *says* that it does. And in our language, it just *doesn't*. We have *another* sentence that says this, namely,

[#] Reality is such that there could have been flying saucers.

This sentence does say that reality is such that there could have been flying saucers, but in our language, [Possible] doesn't. Here's a way to appreciate this. Some people in our community (e.g., certain kinds of mereological nihilists) think that there's no such thing as *reality* because there's no object that's composed of absolutely everything. These people reject [#] because it entails that reality exists. But they don't reject [Possible] because in our language you can say that there's no such thing as reality and still say that there could have been flying saucers. There's no contradiction at all between these two claims in Literese.[36]

"So far we've been telling you what [Possible] *doesn't* say in Literese. We now want to tell you what it *does* say in Literese. It says just what it seems to say – namely, that there could have been flying saucers. This isn't a claim about how things are, but it's still a claim; it's a claim about how things *could have* been. Moreover, the claim that [Possible] makes in our language is a perfectly *objective* claim. When we say that there could have been flying saucers, we're saying something that has nothing at all to do with us or our attitudes or conventions. We're saying, very simply, that there could have been flying saucers, and on our view, this would have been true even if no speakers or thinkers or conventions ever existed.

"Now, you might be thinking that if [Possible] doesn't make a claim about reality, or about how things are, then it doesn't make a *claim* at all. But this stance would make sense only if it were *impossible* to make a claim about how things could have been without making a claim about how things are. But we

---

[36] Note, also, that we don't endorse a <modal nothingist> view of [#]; we think that if [#] true, then it's made true partially by the fact that reality exists.

can't see why anyone would think this is impossible. It seems to us that when we utter [Possible], we just *do* make a claim about how things could have been, and when we do this, we intend to be saying *nothing* about how things are. If this is even possible – and, again, it seems that it is – then we can just *stipulate* that this is what [Possible] does in our language. It makes a claim about how things could have been without making any claim at all about how things are.[37]

"Given that, in our language, [Possible] makes a claim about how things could have been and doesn't make any claim at all about how things are, let us now argue that <modal nothingism> is true of [Possible] – that is, that (i) [Possible] is (substantively and objectively) true in Literese, and (ii) there's nothing about reality that makes it true in Literese.

"Our first argument for claim (i) is based on the fact that (a) flying saucers seem easily conceivable to us, and (b) we have no reason whatsoever to think they're impossible. Given this, we have at least a defeasible prima facie reason to think that flying saucers are possible (in the sense of 'possible' that's at work in our language) and, hence, that [Possible] is true in Literese.

"A second argument for the truth-in-Literese of [Possible] is based on the fact that (a) the claim that there are flying saucers doesn't lead to contradiction, even when we combine it with all of the analytic truths, and (b) glossing over the provisos mentioned in Section 8.2.3, this is sufficient for the sort of possibility that's expressed by the Literese word 'possible.'

"A third argument here is based on the fact that [Possible] is *analytic* in Literese (i.e., that it follows from true claims about what the words in [Possible] mean in Literese).

"A fourth point worth making here – and we admit that this might not count as an actual *argument* – is that it's altogether *obvious* that [Possible] is true in Literese. We've already established that in our language, [Possible] makes a claim about how things could have been. And the point we're making now is that the claim that [Possible] makes in Literese seems – very obviously – to *get things right*. Of *course* there could have been flying saucers. If you denied this, you'd have to say that it's *not the case* that there could have been flying saucers, and that seems extremely implausible.

"Another way to put the point here is as follows: once you've granted that it's possible to make a claim about how things could have been without making

---

[37] We're aware that stipulations about word meanings can fail to succeed – because the meanings of our words are determined not by stipulations, but by our linguistic intentions (where by "our linguistic intentions," we mean all of the (conscious or unconscious) information that's stored in our heads about the meanings of words). But our neuro-cognitive scientists have done extensive research on our linguistic intentions concerning sentences like [Possible], and their findings show that our intentions here line up perfectly with our stipulations.

a claim about how things are, it's hard to see why you would deny that some claims of this kind (e.g., [Possible]) get things *right*, whereas others (e.g., 'There could have been round squares') get things *wrong*. Indeed, it seems completely unreasonable to deny this. For if you do, you'll have to say that it's *not the case* that there could have been flying saucers. And, again, that seems really implausible.[38]

"In any event, given that [Possible] is true in Literese, the next point to note is that [Possible] would be true in Literese no matter what reality was like. It would be true even if there were no such things as possible worlds, or abstract objects, or objects with essences or potentialities. It would be true even if it weren't the case that reality had the property *being such that there could have been flying saucers* because it would be true even if reality didn't exist at all. It would be true even if there were no such things as free-floating modal facts, like *the fact that there could have been flying saucers*. Indeed, [Possible] would be true in our language even if *nothing* existed. Even if there were literally *nothing* – no concrete or abstract objects, no facts, no worlds, no anything – it would still be the case that there could have been flying saucers.

"(We should pause to acknowledge that we're speaking a bit loosely. If nothing existed, then, of course, the sentence [Possible] wouldn't exist, and so it wouldn't be true. Here's a way to make the point non-loosely: if the whole plenitudinous space of Lewisian possible worlds had existed, then *our* sentence [Possible] would have been true *at* (as opposed to *in*) the empty world. But having pointed this out, we'll continue to speak loosely, saying that [Possible] would be true in our language even if nothing existed.[39])

"In any event, it doesn't follow from the fact that [Possible] would be true in our language if nothing existed that there's nothing about reality that makes [Possible] true in our language. After all, [Round or Not Round] would be true if nothing existed, but as we've already seen (in Section 7.3), there's something about reality that makes that sentence true, namely, the fact that Mars is round. But notice that even if nothing existed, there would still be something about

---

[38] Don't read anything into our use of the word 'things' in our claim that [Possible] "gets things right." We're not saying that [Possible] gets something right about *some existing things*. That would be inconsistent with <modal nothingism>. Our claim is simply that [Possible] *is* right and 'There could have been round squares' *isn't* – that is, that there could have been flying saucers but not round squares – and that if you try to deny this, you'll end up having to say things that are extremely implausible.

[39] You might wonder how we know that [Possible] would be true at the empty world – or, for that matter, how we know that the empty world is even possible. This falls out of the stipulation that we're talking here about the broadest kind of possibility (see Section 8.2.4 for more on this). Also, you might think it odd to talk about an empty *Lewisian* world; but since we don't really believe in Lewisian worlds anyway, we can just build it into the fiction that there's an *empty* Lewisian world.

reality that made [Round or Not Round] true; for in that scenario, [Round or Not Round] would be made true by something *not existing*, namely, Mars.[40]

"Anyhow, the point we want to make is this: the reason that [Possible] would be true in our language if nothing existed wouldn't have anything to do with something not existing. The reason [Possible] would be true in our language if nothing existed is exactly the same as the reason that it's true in our language right now. The reason is that the claim that [Possible] makes in our language – the claim it makes about how things could have been – *gets things right*. This is why [Possible] is true in our language right now; this is why [Possible] would be true in our language if nothing existed; and, in fact, no matter what reality was like, this would still be the reason that [Possible] was true in our language.

"These considerations suggest the following argument for the claim that there's nothing about reality that makes [Possible] true in Literese:

> (i) If absolutely *nothing* existed, then [Possible] would be true in Literese, and it would either be made true by something not existing or there would be nothing about reality that made it true (there just don't seem to be any other options). But we just saw that (ii) if nothing existed, then [Possible] wouldn't be made true by something not existing. Therefore, (iii) if nothing existed, then [Possible] would be true in Literese, and there would be nothing about reality that made it true. But we also just saw that (iv) the reason that [Possible] would be true in Literese if nothing existed is exactly the same as the reason that it's true in Literese right now. Therefore, from (iii) and (iv), it follows that (v) right now, there's nothing about reality that makes [Possible] true in Literese.

"A second argument for this conclusion proceeds as follows: Since [Possible] doesn't *say* anything in our language about reality, or about how things *are*, it isn't – and, indeed, *couldn't* be – made true in our language by how things are. How things are – or what reality is like – is completely *irrelevant* to whether [Possible] is true in our language, precisely because [Possible] doesn't *say* anything in our language about how things are.[41] (We're not saying that if a sentence S doesn't make a claim about an object O, then S isn't made true by O; for example, 'There's a red planet in our solar system' doesn't make a claim about Mars, but it's still made true by Mars (and how Mars is). But the only

---

[40] You might doubt that the non-existence of Mars would count as "something about reality"; but even if this were right, it wouldn't undermine our argument; indeed, this would only add more grist to the nothingist mill.

[41] We're talking here about *metaphysical* relevance. We admit that how things are could be *epistemically* relevant (for certain creatures) to the question of whether [Possible] is true in our language. For if there actually *were* flying saucers, then people could use this information to *figure out* that [Possible] is true in our language. But, again, how things are isn't *metaphysically* relevant to whether [Possible] is true in our language.

reason we get this result is that this sentence makes a *nonspecific* claim about how things are. Our claim here is that if a sentence doesn't make *any claim at all* about how things are, then it can't be made true by how things are.)

"A third argument for the claim that there's nothing about reality that makes [Possible] true in Literese is based on the fact that (a) [Possible] makes a claim about how things could have been, and (b) the claim that it makes here – the claim about how things could have been – gets things right. This suggests that [Possible] isn't made true in Literese by reality, or by how things are, because [Possible] is *already* true in Literese; it's true in Literese *before reality enters the picture*, so to speak, because the claim that it makes about how things *could have been* (and *not* about how things *are*) is true.

"So that, in a nutshell, is why we endorse a <modal nothingist> view of our sentence [Possible] – because (a) it's true, and (b) there's nothing about reality that makes it true."

8.5 The Argument for Modal Nothingism

I think the remarks of the Literali make perfect sense. I can't see any reason to think it's impossible to make a claim about how things could have been without making a claim about how things are, and given this, the Literali can just stipulate that that's what they're doing with sentences like [Possible] – or, better, since the Literali are fictional characters, *I* can stipulate that that's what they're doing with sentences like [Possible]. Moreover, I agree with the Literali that once we grant that it's possible to make claims of this kind, it makes little sense to deny that some of these claims (e.g., 'There could have been flying saucers') are right, whereas others (e.g., 'There could have been round squares') are wrong. And, finally, I agree with the Literali's reasons for thinking that there isn't (and *couldn't* be) anything about reality that makes sentences of this kind true.

So I think the Literali's argument for <modal nothingism> is correct. But this means that if I just stipulate that [Possible*] is to function in English* in the same way that [Possible] functions in Literese, then I can steal the Literali's argument for <modal nothingism> and use it as an argument for modal nothingism. And there's no reason why I can't stipulate this; since [Possible*] is my sentence – and since 'possibly*' is my word – I get to say how they function. So this gives us an argument for modal nothingism.

8.6 The Mathematical Anti-Realist's Modal Sentences

I just argued that we can endorse a modal nothingist view of sentences like [Possible*]. But the crucial question for us is whether we can endorse a nothingist view of the modal sentences that mathematical anti-realists are committed to – that is, sentences like the following:

> [CF] If there had actually existed a plenitudinous realm of abstract objects, then it would have been the case that 3 was prime.

> [N] Necessarily, if there exists a plenitudinous realm of abstract objects, then 3 is prime.

I'll discuss [CF] and [N] in a moment. But before I do this, let me first point out that we can endorse a modal nothingist view of sentences like the following:

> [CF*] If there had actually existed a plenitudinous realm of abstract objects, then it would* have been the case that 3 was prime.

> [N*] Necessarily*, if there exists a plenitudinous realm of abstract objects, then 3 is prime.

The reason we can endorse a modal nothingist view of sentences like [CF*] and [N*] is that we can plausibly claim that these sentences are *analytic*, and given the remarks of Section 8.2.2, this means that [CF*] and [N*] are in the domain of sentences that modal nothingism is about. Moreover, just about everything that I said about [Possible*] in Sections 8.2–8.5 carries over, *mutatis mutandis*, to sentences like [CF*] and [N*]. Most importantly, the Literali's argument for <modal nothingism> seems to apply straightforwardly to sentences like [CF*] and [N*].

(In connection with [N*], we have to be careful how we word the argument for modal nothingism. One thing I've said about [Possible*] is that it *doesn't say anything about reality*, or about how things *are*. And we can make an analogous claim about [CF*]. [CF*] doesn't say anything about how things *are*; it makes a claim only about how things *would be* in a certain scenario, and the claim that it makes doesn't depend in any way on how reality actually *is*[42] – which is why it's plausibly taken to be analytic. But you might think that [N*] *does* say something about how things are; for you might think it says that the nonmodal conditional that's embedded in its necessity* operator – that is, 'if there exists a plenitudinous realm of abstract objects, then 3 is prime' – is true. At the very least, we can say that [N*] *entails* this nonmodal conditional, and indeed, it seems that [CF*] entails this conditional as well. But this isn't a problem. Since [CF*] and [N*] aren't *made true* by the fact that makes the nonmodal conditional true – that is, according to mathematical anti-realists, by the fact that abstract objects don't really exist – this doesn't affect the argument for modal

---

[42] I'm aware that the truth values of *some* counterfactuals depend on how reality is (e.g., 'If Madonna had one more car, then she'd have four cars'). My claim is just that the truth values of the counterfactuals that mathematical anti-realists are committed to (e.g., [CF*]) don't depend on how reality is.

nothingism at all, and so we can just note that [CF*] and [N*] have entailments about how things are (and that in connection with [N*], you might think that it *makes a claim* about how things are) and then go on with the argument for a modal nothingist view of [CF*] and [N*].)

So, again, I think that mathematical anti-realists can endorse a modal nothingist view of sentences like [CF*] and [N*]. But what about [CF] and [N]? Well, the first point to note here is that if mathematical anti-realists endorse modal primitivism (i.e., if they endorse the primitivist analysis of ordinary modal discourse), then they can endorse a modal nothingist view of [CF] and [N]. For modal primitivism tells us that ordinary sentences like [CF] and [N] are equivalent to sentences like [CF*] and [N*]; thus, since we just saw that we can endorse a modal nothingist view of [CF*] and [N*], it follows that if modal primitivism is true, then we can endorse a modal nothingist view of [CF] and [N] as well. So if mathematical anti-realists endorse modal primitivism, then they can use modal nothingism to solve the modal truthmaking problem with their view.

But mathematical anti-realists don't have to endorse modal primitivism. For as we saw in Section 6.3, if anti-realists endorse the possible-worlds analysis of ordinary modal discourse – and if they also endorse modal error theory – then the modal truthmaking problem for their view essentially boils down to the need to answer the truthmaking question for sentences like [CF*]. Thus, since (as we've seen in this section) we can endorse a modal nothingist view of sentences like [CF*], it follows that mathematical anti-realists who endorse the possible-worlds analysis of ordinary modal discourse can use modal nothingism to solve the modal truthmaking problem with their view.

8.7 Semantic Neutrality

So far, I've argued that if mathematical anti-realists endorse either modal primitivism or the possible-worlds analysis of ordinary modal discourse, then they can use modal nothingism to solve the modal truthmaking problem with their view. It's worth noting, however, that anti-realists can also endorse Hybrid-Mess-ism – that is, the view that some ordinary modal sentences are best interpreted as involving primitive modal operators and other ordinary modal sentences are best interpreted as involving quantification over possible worlds. Thus, insofar as modal primitivism and the possible-worlds analysis of ordinary modal discourse can both be combined with modal nothingism, it seems to follow that Hybrid-Mess-ism can be combined with that view as well.

Indeed, it seems to me that regardless of whether mathematical anti-realists endorse Hybrid-Mess-ism or modal primitivism or the possible-worlds analysis of ordinary modal discourse, what they're ultimately going to have to do is answer the truthmaking question for sentences like [CF*] or [N*]. Thus, since modal nothingism gives them a way to do this, it follows that mathematical anti-realists can use modal nothingism to solve the modal truthmaking problem with their view, regardless of which of the above three semantic views they endorse.

8.8 A Slight Wrinkle: Applications of Mathematics

We saw in Section 3 that mathematical anti-realists need to account for the applications of mathematics. Moreover, as we saw in Section 3.4.1, one attractive strategy that anti-realists can employ here is to say the same thing about our empirical theories that we say about our mathematical theories, namely, that they're *FAPP-true* – that is, that they would have been true if there had been a plenitude of abstract objects. But if anti-realists endorse this view, then they'll have to commit to the truth of counterfactuals like the following:

> [CF**] If there had actually existed a plenitudinous realm of abstract objects, then it would* have been the case that the air outside was 32 degrees Fahrenheit.

But mathematical anti-realists can handle sentences like this in the same way that modal nothingists handle sentences like [W], [C], and [O] (see Section 8.2.2 for more on this). More specifically, anti-realists can say that [CF**] is made true partially by empirical facts about the air outside and partially by nothing; in particular, anti-realists can say that there's a purely modal part of [CF**] that's made true by nothing.

8.9 Why Modal Nothingism Isn't a Deflationary-Truth View

It might seem that modal nothingism is a deflationary-truth view, but it's not. There are at least three reasons for this. First, modal nothingism doesn't say that sentences of the form '*Fa*' can be true even if the singular term '*a*' doesn't refer. Second, modal nothingism doesn't employ a deflationary concept of truth. Indeed, we could replace the word 'true,' in the formulation of modal nothingism, with the expression 'non-deflationarily true'; that is, we could take modal nothingism to be the view that (a) sentence like [Possible*] and [CF*] are *non-deflationarily true*, and (b) there's nothing about reality that makes them non-deflationarily true. Third, modal nothingism isn't a *conventionalist* view. According to modal nothingism, sentences like [Possible*] and [CF*] are true, and the fact that they're true doesn't have anything to do with our conventions. Or more precisely, *given what these sentences mean*, they're true independently of us and our conventions.[43]

Now, you might wonder how [Possible*] and [CF*] could be true in a non-deflationary, nonconventionalist way, given that there's nothing about reality that makes them true. But I explained how this could be so in Section 8.3; and in Sections 8.4–8.6, I argued that it *is* so. For when I argued that [Possible*] and [CF*] are true and that there's nothing about reality that makes them true, I was talking about non-deflationary, nonconventionalist truth.

---

[43] Unlike modal nothingism, deflationary-truth views *are* conventionalist views. See Section 6.4 for more on this.

References

Armstrong, D. (1997) *A World of States of Affairs*, Cambridge: Cambridge University Press.

Azzouni, J. (2004) *Deflating Existential Consequence: A Case for Nominalism*, Oxford: Oxford University Press.

(2010) *Talking About Nothing*, Oxford: Oxford University Press.

Baker, A. (2005) "Are there Genuine Mathematical Explanations of Physical Phenomena?" *Mind* 114: 223–38.

(2009) "Mathematical Explanation in Science," *British Journal for the Philosophy of Science* 60: 611–33.

Balaguer, M. (1995) "A Platonist Epistemology," *Synthese* 103: 303–25.

(1996) "A Fictionalist Account of the Indispensable Applications of Mathematics," *Philosophical Studies* 83: 291–314.

(1998) *Platonism and Anti-Platonism in Mathematics*, Oxford: Oxford University Press.

(2009) "Fictionalism, Theft, and the Story of Mathematics," *Philosophia Mathematica* 17: 131–62.

(2010) "Fictionalism, Mathematical Facts, and Logical Facts," in *Fictions and Models*, J. Woods (ed.), Munich: Philosophia Verlag, pp. 149–89.

(2014) "A Guide for the Perplexed: What Mathematicians Need to Know to Understand Philosophers of Mathematics," *The Mathematical Intelligencer* 36: 3–8.

(2016) "Full-Blooded Platonism," in *An Historical Introduction to the Philosophy of Mathematics*, R. Marcus and M. McEvoy (eds.), London: Bloomsbury Press, pp. 719–32.

(2021) *Metaphysics, Sophistry, and Illusion: Toward a Widespread Non-Factualism*, Oxford: Oxford University Press.

Benacerraf, P. (1973) "Mathematical Truth," *Journal of Philosophy* 70: 661–79.

Bernstein, S. (2016) "Omission Impossible," *Philosophical Studies* 173: 2575–89.

Berto, F., French, R., Priest, G., and Ripley, D. (2018) "Williamson on Counterpossibles," *Journal of Philosophical Logic* 47: 693–713.

Bjerring, J. C. (2014) "On Counterpossibles," *Philosophical Studies* 168: 327–53.

Boghossian, P. (1997) "Analyticity," in *A Companion to the Philosophy of Language*, B. Hale and C. Wright (eds.), Oxford: Blackwell, pp. 331–68.

Brogaard, B. and Salerno, J. (2013) "Remarks on Counterpossibles," *Synthese* 190: 639–60.

Brouwer, L. E. J. (1983a [1912]) "Intuitionism and Formalism," in *Philosophy of Mathematics*, P. Benacerraf and H. Putnam (eds.), Cambridge: Cambridge University Press, pp. 77–89.

(1983b [1948]) "Consciousness, Philosophy, and Mathematics," in *Philosophy of Mathematics*, P. Benacerraf and H. Putnam (eds.), Cambridge: Cambridge University Press, pp. 90–96.

Bueno, O. (2005) "Dirac and the Dispensability of Mathematics," *Studies in History and Philosophy of Modern Physics* 36: 465–90.

(2009) "Mathematical Fictionalism," in *New Waves in Philosophy of Mathematics*, O. Bueno and Ø. Linnebo (eds.), Basingstoke: Palgrave Macmillan, pp. 59–79.

Bueno, O. and Shalkowski, S. (2009) "Modalism and Logical Pluralism," *Mind* 118: 295–321.

Cameron, R. (2009a) "What's Metaphysical about Metaphysical Necessity?" *Philosophy and Phenomenological Research* 79: 1–16.

(2009b) "Truthmakers and Modality," *Synthese* 164: 261–80.

Chihara, C. (1990) *Constructibility and Mathematical Existence*, Oxford: Oxford University Press.

Colyvan, M. (2001) *The Indispensability of Mathematics*, Oxford: Oxford University Press.

Dodd, J. (2002) "Is Truth Supervenient on Being," *Proceedings of the Aristotelian Society* 102: 69–85.

Dorr, C. (2008) "There Are No Abstract Objects," in *Contemporary Debates in Metaphysics*, T. Sider, J. Hawthorne, and D. Zimmerman (eds.), Oxford: Blackwell, pp. 12–64.

Field, H. (1980) *Science without Numbers*, Princeton, NJ: Princeton University Press.

(1989) *Realism, Mathematics, and Modality*, Oxford: Blackwell.

(1998) "Mathematical Objectivity and Mathematical Objects," in *Contemporary Readings in the Foundations of Metaphysics*, C. MacDonald and S. Laurence (eds.), Oxford: Blackwell, pp. 387–403.

Fine, K. (1994) "Essence and Modality: The Second Philosophical Perspectives Lecture," *Philosophical Perspectives* 8: 1–16.

(2005) *Modality and Tense*, Oxford: Oxford University Press.

Forbes, G. (1985) *The Metaphysics of Modality*, Oxford: Clarendon Press.

(1989) *Languages of Possibility*, Oxford: Blackwell.

Frege, G. (1953 [1884]) *The Foundations of Arithmetic*, J. L. Austin (trans.), Oxford: Blackwell.

(1964 [1893–1903]) *The Basic Laws of Arithmetic*, M. Furth (trans.), Berkeley: University of California Press.

(1980) *Philosophical and Mathematical Correspondence*, Chicago: University of Chicago Press.

Gödel, K. (1983 [1964]) "What Is Cantor's Continuum Problem?" in *Philosophy of Mathematics*, P. Benacerraf and H. Putnam (eds.), Cambridge: Cambridge University Press, pp. 470–85.

Hellman, G. (1989) *Mathematics Without Numbers*, Oxford: Clarendon Press.

Heyting, A. (1956) *Intuitionism*, Amsterdam: North-Holland.

Hilbert, D. (1959 [1899]) *Foundations of Geometry*, E. Townsend (trans.), La Salle, IL: Open Court.

Hofweber, T. (2005) "Number Determiners, Numbers, and Arithmetic," *Philosophical Review* 114: 179–225.

Horgan, T. (1984) "Science Nominalized," *Philosophy of Science* 51: 529–49.

Kitcher, P. (1984) *The Nature of Mathematical Knowledge*, Oxford: Oxford University Press.

Kripke, S. (1980) *Naming and Necessity*, Cambridge, MA: Harvard University Press.

Leng, M. (2010) *Mathematics and Reality*, Oxford: Oxford University Press.

Lewis, D. (1986) *On the Plurality of Worlds*, Oxford: Blackwell.

(1991) *Parts of Classes*, Oxford: Blackwell.

(1992) "Armstrong on Combinatorial Possibility," *Australasian Journal of Philosophy* 70: 211–24.

Lewy, C. (1976) *Meaning and Modality*, Cambridge: Cambridge University Press.

Lowe, E. J. (n.d.) "Metaphysics as the Science of Essence." Unpublished manuscript.

Ludwig, K. (n.d.) "De Re Necessities." Unpublished manuscript.

Maddy, P. (1990) *Realism in Mathematics*, Oxford: Oxford University Press.

Mares, E. D. and Fuhrmann, A. (1995) "A Relevant Theory of Conditionals," *Journal of Philosophical Logic* 24: 645–65.

Meinong, A. (1904) "Ueber Gegenstandstheorie," in *Untersuchungen zur Gegenstandstheorie und Psychologie*, A. Meinong (ed.), Leipzig: Barth, pp. 1–51.

Melia, J. (2000) "Weaseling Away the Indispensability Argument," *Mind* 109: 455–79.

Mill, J. S. (1843) *A System of Logic*, London: Longmans, Green, and Company.

Moltmann, F. (2013) "Reference to Numbers in Natural Language," *Philosophical Studies* 162: 499–536.

Nolan, D. (1997) "Impossible Worlds: A Modest Approach," *Notre Dame Journal of Formal Logic* 38: 535–72.

Parsons, J. (1999) "There Is No 'Truthmaker' Argument Against Nominalism," *Australasian Journal of Philosophy* 77: 325–34.

Plantinga, A. (1976) "Actualism and Possible Worlds," *Theoria* 42: 139–60.

Priest, G. (2003) "Meinongianism and the Philosophy of Mathematics," *Philosophia Mathematica* 11: 3–15.

(2005) *Towards Non-Being*, Oxford: Oxford University Press.

Putnam, H. (1967) "The Thesis That Mathematics Is Logic," in *Bertrand Russell, Philosopher of the Century*, R. Schoenman (ed.), London: Allen and Unwin, pp. 273–303.

(1971) *Philosophy of Logic*, New York: Harper and Row.

(1983 [1967]) "Mathematics without Foundations," in *Philosophy of Mathematics*, 2nd ed., P. Benacerraf and H. Putnam (eds.), Cambridge: Cambridge University Press, . pp. 295–311.

Quine, W. V. O. (1983 [1936]) "Truth by Convention," in *Philosophy of Mathematics*, 2nd ed., P. Benacerraf and H. Putnam (eds.), Cambridge: Cambridge University Press, pp. 329–54.

(1961a [1948]) "On What There Is," in *From a Logical Point of* View, 2nd ed., New York: Harper and Row, pp. 1–19.

(1961b [1951]) "Two Dogmas of Empiricism," in *From a Logical Point of* View, 2nd ed., New York: Harper and Row, pp. 20–46.

Rayo, A. (2008) "On Specifying Truth-Conditions," *Philosophical Review* 117: 385–443.

(2013) *The Construction of Logical Space*, Oxford: Oxford University Press.

Resnik, M. (1980) *Frege and the Philosophy of Mathematics*, Ithaca, NY: Cornell University Press.

(1997) *Mathematics as a Science of Patterns*, Oxford: Oxford University Press.

Rosen, G. (1990) "Modal Fictionalism," *Mind* 99: 327–54.

(2001) "Nominalism, Naturalism, Epistemic Relativism," in *Philosophical Topics* XV (Metaphysics), J. Tomberlin (ed.), Malden, MA: Blackwell, pp. 60–91.

Routley, R. (1980) *Exploring Meinong's Jungle and Beyond*, Canberra: RSSS, Australian National University.

Russell, B. (1903) *Principles of Mathematics*, Cambridge: Cambridge University Press.

Shalkowski, S. (1994) "The Ontological Ground of Alethic Modality," *Philosophical Review* 103: 669–88.

Shapiro, S. (1997) *Philosophy of Mathematics: Structure and Ontology*, New York: Oxford University Press.

Sidelle, A. (1989) *Necessity, Essence, and Individuation*, Ithaca, NY: Cornell University Press.

Sider, T. (2003) "Reductive Theories of Modality," in *The Oxford Handbook of Metaphysics*, M. Loux and D. Zimmerman (eds.), Oxford: Oxford University Press, pp. 180–208.

(2011) *Writing the Book of the World*, Oxford: Clarendon Press.

Stalnaker, R. (1976) "Possible Worlds," *Nous* 10: 65–75.

Strawson, P. F. (1950) "On Referring," *Mind* 59: 320–44.

Tallant, J. (2009) "Ontological Cheats Might Just Prosper," *Analysis* 69: 422–30.

Thomasson, A. (2009) "Non-Descriptivism about Modality: A Brief History and Revival," *Baltic International Yearbook of Cognition, Logic, and Communication* 4: 1–26.

(2020) *Norms and Necessity*, Oxford: Oxford University Press.

Vetter, B. (2018) *Potentiality: From Dispositions to Modality*, Oxford: Oxford University Press.

Warren, J. (2015) "The Possibility of Truth by Convention," *Philosophical Quarterly* 65: 84–93.

Williamson, T. (2007) *The Philosophy of Philosophy*, Oxford: Blackwell.

Wittgenstein, L. (1956) *Remarks on the Foundations of Mathematics*, Oxford: Blackwell.

Yablo, S. (2002a) "Go Figure: A Path Through Fictionalism," *Midwest Studies in Philosophy* 25: 72–102.

(2002b) "Abstract Objects: A Case Study," *Noûs* 36 (Supplementary Volume 1): 220–40.

(2005) "The Myth of the Seven," in *Fictionalism in Metaphysics*, M. Kalderon (ed.), New York: Oxford University Press, pp. 88–115.

(2017) "If-Thenism," *Australasian Philosophical Review* 1: 115–32.

Zalta, E. (1999) "Natural Numbers and Natural Cardinals as Abstract Objects: A Partial Reconstruction of Frege's *Grundgesetze* in Object Theory," *Journal of Philosophical Logic* 28: 619–60.

Cambridge Elements $\equiv$

The Philosophy of Mathematics

Penelope Rush

University of Tasmania

From the time Penny Rush completed her thesis in the philosophy of mathematics (2005), she has worked continuously on themes around the realism/anti-realism divide and the nature of mathematics. Her edited collection *The Metaphysics of Logic* (Cambridge University Press, 2014), and forthcoming essay 'Metaphysical Optimism' (*Philosophy Supplement*), highlight a particular interest in the idea of reality itself and curiosity and respect as important philosophical methodologies.

Stewart Shapiro

The Ohio State University

Stewart Shapiro is the O'Donnell Professor of Philosophy at The Ohio State University, a Distinguished Visiting Professor at the University of Connecticut, and a Professorial Fellow at the University of Oslo. His major works include *Foundations without Foundationalism* (1991), *Philosophy of Mathematics: Structure and Ontology* (1997), *Vagueness in Context* (2006), and *Varieties of Logic* (2014). He has taught courses in logic, philosophy of mathematics, metaphysics, epistemology, philosophy of religion, Jewish philosophy, social and political philosophy, and medical ethics.

About the Series

This Cambridge Elements series provides an extensive overview of the philosophy of mathematics in its many and varied forms. Distinguished authors will provide an up-to-date summary of the results of current research in their fields and give their own take on what they believe are the most significant debates influencing research, drawing original conclusions.

Printed in the United States
by Baker & Taylor Publisher Services